Raise Your Kids to Succeed

Other Books by Chris Palmer

Now What, Grad? Your Path to Success After College (Rowman &
Littlefield, 2016)

*Confessions of a Wildlife Filmmaker: The Challenges of Staying Honest in
an Industry Where Ratings Are King* (Bluefield Publishing, 2015)

*Shooting in the Wild: An Insider's Account of Making Movies in the Animal
Kingdom* (Sierra Club Books, 2010)

~

All proceeds from the sale of this book will go to fund scholarships for students
at American University School of Communication

Raise Your Kids to Succeed

What Every Parent Should Know

Chris Palmer

ROWMAN & LITTLEFIELD

Lanham • Boulder • New York • London

Published by Rowman & Littlefield
A wholly owned subsidiary of The Rowman & Littlefield Publishing Group, Inc.
4501 Forbes Boulevard, Suite 200, Lanham, Maryland 20706
www.rowman.com

Unit A, Whitacre Mews, 26–34 Stannary Street, London SE11 4AB

British Library Cataloguing-in-Publication Information Available

Library of Congress Cataloging-in-Publication Data Available

ISBN: 978-1-4758-2983-9 (cloth : alk. paper)
ISBN: 978-1-4758-2984-6 (pbk. : alk. paper)
ISBN: 978-1-4758-2985-3 (electronic)

∞™ The paper used in this publication meets the minimum requirements of American National Standard for Information Sciences—Permanence of Paper for Printed Library Materials, ANSI/NISO Z39.48–1992.

Printed in the United States of America

Dedicated to my wonderful family: Gail, Kimberly, Sujay, Christina, CJ, Jenny, Chase, Kareena, Neal, Jackson, and Max. I have learned to be a better parent from you.
And also dedicated to my loving parents, Mavis and Sidney John Palmer.

Contents

Preface

When my wife, Gail, and I decided to start a family, I knew nothing about raising children. I was, however, aware that they could be obstreperous, demanding, and stress-inducing. As the youngest of four boys, I had experienced a rather stressful childhood myself. I feared that by becoming a parent I might be condemning myself to a life of anxiety, struggle, and regret. But more than anything, I was terrified of failing. I wanted my kids to be happy and successful.

Despite my misgivings, we forged ahead and gave birth to three daughters.

Working diligently to build my career as a wildlife filmmaker meant traveling extensively and spending a lot of time away from my family. At home, I wanted to be a capable, loving, and effective father, but the girls sometimes kept me at a distance. I recall one night when Gail and I put our daughters to bed and I tried to cuddle with each one.

"Would you like to snuggle?" I asked my girls, all of them under ten years of age and each of them adorable, loving, and beautiful in her own way. "No," they answered, one by one, unknowingly inflicting wounds to my heart. They would only snuggle with their mom. It hurt to be left out.

Full of self-doubt and worried that I was failing as a father, I wondered whether my own father had ever felt the same way. I suddenly had a new understanding of the difficulties he might have experienced as a parent.

I wanted to be a better father and I wondered if I was devoting sufficient time to parenting. For a month, I kept a log of everything I did during the day and how long it took me. I discovered a massive discrepancy between how I spent my time and what I claimed was important to me. I would glibly tell people that my family was my top priority but, when I analyzed my schedule, I found that I devoted 90 percent of my time to my job. I was a workaholic.

I yearned to be a father who wasn't simply an awkward appendage to the nuclear group, but a pivotal and integrated member. The feelings of rejection roiling inside me prompted me to start thinking of innovative things I could do to play a more significant and meaningful role in my daughters' lives.

I became a student of what makes an effective parent. I resolved to learn all I could about what it means to be a loving and capable father. I undertook a deliberate, self-imposed program of study, reading book after book on parenting.

I also took every opportunity to talk to other fathers about what they did and didn't do, and what they found worked and didn't work. And, of course, I observed other families and drew my own conclusions about which fathering behaviors produced good results and which ones didn't.

One of my first insights was that fathering was a skill I could learn (like cooking or playing golf), not something that just happened to a man when he had children. It wasn't a fixed, inborn talent, but rather something that could be taught, acquired, implemented, and constantly improved upon. Great parents are made, not born.

Inspired by my studies of parenting, and with Gail's support, I introduced new traditions to help build a strong family and set up our kids to succeed.

One idea that I fell in love with was creating "family rituals"—constructive things we would do as a family that our children could rely on to happen, so that they would grow up with a strong sense of rootedness, love, and trust.

When children know that there are certain things they can count on, they feel more confident that they can excel in the world rather than be defeated by it. Our children knew that they could always come home for support, encouragement, and guidance. They knew they would be safe. Whatever madness was happening in the world, our children knew their family was a secure place of trust, sanity, and love.

Unfortunately, not all of my attempts to create rituals worked out. I could never get my daughters to buy into the idea of a regular "Date with Dad," during which I would spend one-on-one time with a daughter during an evening doing anything she wanted.

One successful idea I came up with was to write letters to my daughters every night when I was away traveling and making films. I invested a lot of time and effort in these letters, and wrote hundreds of them over the years. I saw that my daughters really liked them and got a lot out of them. The letters were a way I could build a meaningful connection with my children. I wrote to them about all sorts of things, such as how to give a dinner party, the importance of having a rich vocabulary, and stories about Abraham Lincoln and George Washington.

When I was away from home, my nightly letters were an attempt to get the attention of my daughters and not be "out of sight, out of mind." I soon realized that the letters were a wonderful way to tell my daughters things and pass on knowledge, love, and wisdom that I might find difficult to do face-to-face. Like a lot of men, I wasn't very good at expressing my feelings. I found it easier to do in letters.

Another family ritual was to hold a weekly family meeting with a written agenda. Our family members took turns chairing and running the meetings, which usually lasted about half an hour. The agenda would contain perhaps fifteen items relating to family matters, such as upcoming vacations, organizing the trips for the next day's multiple soccer games, deciding how to organize chores more fairly, going over New Year's resolutions, providing "encouragement" and sharing "rocks."

The "rocks" agenda item involved each family member stating the one or two most important projects she faced in the coming week, such as taking an exam, repairing a frayed relationship, or completing an unfinished task.

The "encouragement" agenda item was important. During "encouragement," everyone in the family, in turn, offered encouragement (not necessarily praise) to every member of the family for doing "something right."

For example, I might say, "Kim, you worked really hard on that calculus homework last night and I commend you for that." Or, "Tina, you lost the tennis match 0–8 but you didn't give up and kept focused until the end."

Encouragement is a mechanism to get everyone to focus on what is going *right* in the family. The point was to avoid the natural tendency in people and families to focus on what is going *wrong*.

My daughters often resisted these family meetings, but I insisted. They enabled us to communicate more effectively. They helped to maintain order in what otherwise could have been a chaotic household. And they gave our daughters the experience of organizing and leading meetings.

Here are eleven other successful rituals and traditions we developed in my family:

1. Over about a nine-month period when my children were young, we created a Family Mission Statement. (See the box at the end of this preface.) Everyone contributed to it. We then framed it and hung it on the wall in a prominent place in the house, so it would be a constant reminder to us all.

2. Every year on January 1, we each wrote our goals for the coming year. I collected them all and made copies for everyone, so that we all knew each other's goals and could help each other achieve them. My daughters are in their late 20s and 30s now, but I still collect everyone's New Year resolutions!

3. I keep a family journal, and every Christmas Day I give each member of the family a book of about 200–300 pages chronicling everything of interest that has gone on in the family that year.

4. We started a "predictions" tradition, in which every member of the family makes a secret prediction on January 1 for the coming year. On the following Christmas Day, we open the sealed envelopes and see how accurate the predictions have been. As we go around the table, smiles and laughter fill the room.

5. On each child's birthday, I hid dollars around the family room equal in number to their age, such as twelve dollar bills on a twelfth birthday.

6. Also on their birthdays, I developed a treasure hunt for each birthday gift. Following funny, cryptic clues, often poems, the birthday girl went around the house to find the hidden gifts.

7. I often bought T-shirts for the whole family with a family photo on them, or with the words "The Shearer-Palmer Family" emblazoned across the front.

8. I did science experiments regularly with my daughters (more on that in chapter 9).

9. I took my daughters on filming trips to Alaska, Tahiti, Barbados, the Bahamas, and other fun and educational places. While the "Date with Dad" idea may have fizzled, I found other ways to spend time one-on-one with the girls.

10. I instigated daily sessions of something I called "teacher/student," in which my kids and I would reverse roles and they became the teacher. They could pick any topic (usually something they had learned in school) and had to teach it to me.

11. Finally, a crucially important thing I had to learn was how to say, "I love you." I learned from a book on fathering that it was important for children to hear their dads say that to them. I disciplined myself to say it. It wasn't easy.

Despite my efforts to be a good dad, I still tripped up. I would sometimes lose my temper. I remember—to my undying shame—going to the basement one evening with our gentle middle daughter, Christina, to help her hammer nails into a piece of wood for a science experiment. She was perhaps six or seven years old—a quiet, reflective, sensitive child. After she missed nail after nail with the hammer, I rashly snatched the hammer from her and finished the project myself.

Later, remorse washed over me as I realized how ugly and toxic my impatience had been. The stress I had been feeling from work challenges was hanging over me and had narrowed my patience to a sliver. Still, that was no excuse for my behavior. I resolved to do better. I *had* to do better if I wanted my family to be happy and healthy. My first step was to apologize to Christina. "Sweetie, will you forgive me?" Of course, the loving little girl that she was, she said that she would.

Soon after this regrettable incident, I read Stephen R. Covey's book *The Seven Habits of Highly Effective People*. One idea in the book was, for me, a life-changing revelation. Covey said that one should never lose one's temper or get irritable. It never does any good. It accomplishes nothing and only sows mistrust and fear. I stared at his words and read them over and over. "If that is true—and I know it to be true," I said to myself, "why would I ever be irascible, snappish, and ill-tempered again? It makes no sense." After that leap of understanding, I very rarely, if ever, lost my temper and, when I did, it was never to the same degree. Over time, I could feel the trust growing in everyone around me—my children included.

It took several years of relentless self-discipline and study of self-improvement books to rid myself totally of the temptation to succumb to irritability. I realized it was a profoundly destructive habit. My impatience achieved nothing, eroded my family's trust in me, and made my daughters feel as though they were walking on eggshells. I learned that the opposite of irritability isn't meekness or passivity, but attentive listening. Listening actively to other people makes losing one's temper impossible.

As I gained the skills to be a better father, I learned to apply those same skills to my professional work. This helped me become a better filmmaker, because my leadership abilities improved. I kept my promises, made more of them, and spoke more clearly. I listened more actively and was kinder. I became more self-aware and less self-absorbed. All of the qualities that made a good father also made for a good leader. I slowly learned to live more intentionally—to decide what person I wanted to be and to commit to achieving that goal, acknowledging that I will forever be a work in progress.

Despite my initial worries about having kids, it turned out that having children was the best and wisest decision I ever made. My daughters were a joy to raise. Kim is now a journalist and a published book author, Christina a doctor, and Jenny a lawyer.

All three are loving and affectionate beyond words, and I learn from them constantly. For example, they recently taught me the power of a plant-based diet to avoid disease and live a healthy, robust long life.

My children bring extraordinary meaning and purpose to my life. They helped move me from being a selfish, egocentric male to a person who is more sensitive and open to listening; more willing to apologize for mistakes; and more loving, empathetic, and generous. My daughters have brought out the best in me, and I hope that Gail and I have done the same for them.

* * *

I approached writing this book from two complementary angles: as a parent who raised three children and as a professor who teaches young adults. As a father, this is the book I wish I had read when I was starting out as a naïve and inexperienced parent many years ago. As a professor, I am acutely aware that if parents did a better job, their kids would be much better prepared for college. Professors like me would be able to achieve so much more with their sons and daughters while they are at college.

I want to see freshmen arriving at college—resilient, confident, self-disciplined, ethical, conscientious, and ambitious. This book shows how you can raise such children by being loving, firm, kind, and capable. Better parenting means better students for professors like me.

Don't worry about not being a perfect parent. None of us is. In writing this book, I have deepened my own understanding of parenting—what works and what doesn't work. I remain, however, a fellow learner, and I continue to make mistakes. The best parents are constantly trying to improve and never are completely satisfied with what they have achieved.

All parents struggle to do well. Even the best parents don't find it easy and have bad days, during which frustration levels hit the ceiling and judgment fails in some way. This goes with the territory.

Raising happy and fulfilled children who succeed at whatever they put their minds to, and who deal coolly with defeats and setbacks, is enormously fulfilling. Taking responsibility for your child's learning and education is one of the noblest tasks you as a parent can perform. It leaves a rich legacy for future generations.

SHEARER-PALMER FAMILY MISSION STATEMENT

November 1990

The mission of our family is to create a nurturing place of love, laughter, warmth, security, relaxation, and happiness, and to provide opportunities for each of us to meet our full potential so that we can each make a positive contribution both to our own family life and to society.

Among these goals are to love each other; to help each other; to believe in each other; to encourage each other; and to wisely use our time, talents, and resources.

We want to live our lives with integrity, courage, humility, love, justice, patience, humor, trust, loyalty, self-confidence, hard work, and self-discipline.

We want our home environment to be warm, and to provide a place where we all feel relaxed and happy, and which warmly welcomes our friends and relatives.

As parents, we want our children to gain from their family life not only their roots but their wings. We want them to feel the special bond that pulls them back home to spend time with their family, but also to understand who they are, based on what we know and can learn about grandparents and relatives who went before them. We want them to develop faith in themselves so that they will work hard in school and know that, with hard work and self-confidence, the world is theirs and they can achieve great things.

Bringing these goals to a day-to-day level:

- We not only want to have time to be with our friends, but also to save time to spend together doing things as a family. And we should have some time to just relax and do things around the house

- We want always to be loving to each other

- We want to be happy

- We want each of us to have a love of learning

- We want each of us to remember people who are not as fortunate as we are, and to find concrete (even if small) ways to help them

- We want to exercise wisdom in what we choose to eat, read, see, and how we spend our time

- We should remember to be generous with our hugs (everyone needs at least ten a day!)

- No matter how pressing our work or school challenges, we should always remember that a happy family life is of prime importance, and demands a lot of our time and attention. "Quality time" isn't enough!

- We will have weekly family meetings, plan memorable and exciting vacations, and keep fit and healthy

- We should all be patient with each other

- We should all be sensitive to each other's feelings

We are lucky to have each other. We should remember this each day!

Acknowledgments

This book is a practical, concise manual for busy parents who don't have time to read a long book on parenting.

Sprinkled throughout are more than fifty stories written by others about what their parents did to help them succeed. I am grateful to the many friends and colleagues who shared their parenting stories with me. These stories illustrate the creativity, love, and wisdom that so many parents exhibit day in and day out.

The contributors are Ben Beach, Jared Beck, Katie Bryden, Jim Bullard, Alicia Burgess, Alexandra Bennett Cannady, Nelson Cooney, Anna Cummins, Mike Dante, Sujay Davé, Aditi Desai, Susan DeVico, Sirjaut Kaur Dhariwal, Erica Dominitz, Kakky Dye, Bailey Edelstein, Berna Elibuyuk, Laura Gamse, Bill Gentile, Sean Gilfillan, Vanina Harel, Elizabeth Herzfeldt-Kamprath, Ashley Holmes, Elaina Kimes, Megan King, Karl Klontz, Alex Korba, Emma Kouguell, Shannon Lawrence, Alison Leithner, Diane MacEachern, David Mullins, Christina Palmer, Jenny Palmer, Kimberly Palmer, Nick Papadis, Elizabeth Ruml, Chuck Saltsman, Crystal Solberg, Ana Sotelo, Tam Sackman, Sara Pereira da Silva, Rick Stack, Scott Talan, Kent Wagner, Phil Warburg, Alexandria Ward, Sam Whitcraft, Carlton John Willey, Mackenzie Yaryura, and Alexandra Yingst. Thank you all!

I will be forever indebted to the many doctors, social scientists, and other parenting experts who have inspired my thinking on parenting, including Dr. Leonard Sax, the late Jeffrey Zaslow, Dr. Catherine Steiner-Adair, Dr. Wendy Mogel, Kim John Payne, Dr. Mary Pipher, Paul Lewis, Jennifer Senior, Don Dinkmeyer, Gary McKay, Meg Meeker, Drs. Myra and David Sadker, Dorothy Rich, Adele Faber, Elaine Mazlish, Joe Kelly, Dr. Carol Gilligan, Marguerite Kelly, Wayne Parker, Katherine Lee, Amy Morin, Sherri Gordon, Lisa Linnell-Olson, Vicki Abeles, Meghan Leahy, the late

Stephen R. Covey, and Dr. Michael Schwartz. I'm deeply grateful to each of them. Their wisdom is reflected on every page of this book, and I cite them frequently. I thank them for their contributions.

I also thank Dr. Ben Stokes and Dr. Lindsay Grace for reviewing chapter 11 on screen time and videogames.

My youngest daughter, Jenny, played a big role in helping me think through how to organize the book. My wife, Gail, and my daughters Kimberly and Christina gave me important criticism on early drafts. Wendy A. Jordan did a superb job editing the text. My colleagues at American University, including Sirjaut Dhariwal, Elizabeth Herzfeldt-Kamprath, Crystal Solberg, Kent Wagner, and Sam Sheline, gave me useful feedback.

My writing friends, in particular authors John Burgess, Roger DiSilvestro, and Diane MacEachern, gave me constant support and help.

Huge appreciation to the whole team at Rowman & Littlefield, but most especially to Tom Koerner, for believing in this book and publishing it.

My family is a continual source of joy and inspiration. I'm deeply grateful to my wonderful wife, my three amazing daughters, my three outstanding sons-in-law (Sujay, CJ, and Chase), and my four adorable grandchildren (Kareena, Neal, Jackson, and Max).

All proceeds from this book will go to fund scholarships for students at American University, where I teach.

Introduction: Whom This Book
Is for and How to Use It

When I became a dad for the first time in 1979, I quickly learned that there was no clear instruction guide for fathers. As I explained in the preface, I made lots of mistakes.

I wrote this book to address a gap identified recently by parenthood expert Jennifer Senior. In her book *All Joy and No Fun*, she observed that parents nowadays pour huge amounts of emotional and financial capital into their children, "yet parents don't know what it is they are supposed to *do*."[1]

In very practical terms, *Raising Your Kids to Succeed: What Every Parent Should Know* describes exactly what parents can do to be effective and help their children succeed.

I have directed this book to parents, but its content is also relevant to teachers and students. It will help any reader who is looking for guidance on what parents can do to help their kids thrive and enjoy school, and then go on to lifelong success. It covers how to create a strong foundation for learning at home, how to give children a strong start, how to support them at school, and how to work with teachers and schools.

Although the chapters build on one another and are arranged in a sequence designed to give a certain order to actions and behavior that make an effective parent, you can jump into the book at any point. You will find that the chapters largely stand alone, offering advice on critical aspects of parenting.

Part I: *Create a Strong Foundation for Learning* opens with some big, foundational questions, including the need for parents to realize their own importance. It goes on to discuss how to create a family mission statement, the importance of creating family traditions and rituals, and the pivotal need to model good behavior. Part I ends with a chapter on how to exert wise discipline and responsibility.

Part II: *Give Your Child a Head Start at Home* starts by exploring ways to let your kids know the importance you attach to education. It stresses the importance of really listening to your kids, reading to them, doing science experiments with them, getting outside with them to enjoy nature, and teaching them life skills. The section ends by giving practical advice on how to control and limit screen time.

Part III: *Support Your Child at School* explores ways for you to be present at your child's school and to be an advocate for your child. This section offers advice on how to help with homework and how to help your child prepare for tests. Chapters 16 and 17 focus on the issue of bullying (including cyberbullying) and how to counter a toxic, sexualized, and violent culture, both issues that can impede your child's learning in school. Finally, chapter 18 looks at the bigger picture and asks a fundamental question: What is the reason kids go to school? Is it all about grades?

I hope you find *Raise Your Kids to Succeed* to be a useful guide as you chart your course through the challenges of raising children. I also hope that this book provides the support that helps your children succeed and reach all of the dreams that you have for them—and, more important, the ones they have for themselves.

Part I

CREATE A STRONG FOUNDATION FOR LEARNING

Chapter 1

Realize Your Importance

Being a successful parent doesn't just happen. It takes desire, study, practice, struggle, planning, determination, and diligence. Above all, it takes grasping your importance as a parent and taking your parenting responsibilities seriously.

Helping your child succeed in life, as well as in school, starts the day that child is born. The stronger, more loving, and more secure your relationship is with her, the more you'll be able to help her succeed. You want her to succeed in school to plant roots so she can grow up to be fulfilled, happy, and successful at whatever career or way of life she decides to pursue.

Family research suggests that children who have devoted, loving, competent parents are more likely to feel self-confident, be assertive, do better in school and in their careers, and feel good about themselves.

BEN BEACH

My mother drove home the value of education by example. She loved to read, so we would see her on the living room couch reading a history book. She volunteered at school, and several of the elementary school teachers, my brother, and I had become lifelong friends of my parents. (My first-grade teacher traveled 200 miles to attend my wedding.) Mom also was an active college alumna, and I remember the college president visiting our home. The importance—and fun—of education was crystal clear.

We also saw Mom writing a lot. She kept a diary, wrote many notes and cards to friends, and recorded all kinds of information in the "baby books" she kept on all four of her children. It's probably no surprise that both my brother and I chose writing careers.

Of course, Mom read bedtime stories to us, although it was not unusual for Dad to tell us stories that he created on the spot.

Finally, and perhaps most important, she built up my self-confidence. She took an interest in my schoolwork and other activities, praised my efforts, and complimented me on any successes. A lot of my own behavior as a parent is modeled on hers.

Here are twenty-five "best parenting practices" to build a strong and supportive relationship with your kids:

1. *Be a role model.* Children should see parents who are physically, mentally, and emotionally healthy, so that they have a positive example to emulate. Moreover, daughters who spend time with a loving and capable father—and sons who spend time with a loving and capable mother—know what to look for in a life partner and know that she (your adult child) deserves to be treated respectfully. Every mother and father should manifest what it is to be a responsible and trustworthy person by being kind, courteous, respectful, and honest.

2. *Be a teacher and coach.* Skilled parents teach their kids to know right from wrong, to make good choices and to grasp basic life lessons, such as how to be resilient and rebound from setbacks and disappointments. They look for teaching moments to help their children become independent and self-reliant.

3. *Teach values and principles.* Identify your own core values and timeless principles and live by them. Know what matters deeply to you and share those ideals with your family while modeling them in your daily life and actions. Great parents pass on values and principles to their children, who navigate in a world sometimes bereft of them.

4. *Respect your child's other parent.* If you are married, keep your marriage strong and vibrant. If you're not married, respect and support your child's other parent. Never demean or belittle the other parent. When your child sees his parents behaving in a caring and respectful way toward each other, he is more likely to feel secure and accepted. Parents need to cooperate, not compete or fight with each other.

5. *Spend time with your child.* It is essential to spend quality time with your children and not neglect them. It can be challenging to have quality time without spending quantity time. If carving out time to be with your children means not playing golf on the weekend, so be it. Sacrificing nonessentials is a key way to show you are a committed parent. Spending time with your child shows you love and value her. You don't want to grow old and regret having missed opportunities to do things together. Those opportunities, once gone, are gone forever. Give your child ample time with you so that she will be less likely to seek inappropriate attention from other adults or influences.

6. *Eat together as a family.* Eating dinner together with the family every evening gives your child a chance to talk about the good and not-so-good things that happened to him during the day. It also gives you the chance to listen and, when appropriate, offer support or advice.

7. *Read to your child.* Instilling in your child a deep love of reading and of books is one of the most powerful things you can do to lay the groundwork for her success at school and in life.

8. *Be affectionate.* Daughters and sons need the security that comes from knowing they are adored by their parents, and that their parents love being close to them. Give gentle hugs, kisses on the cheek, and an arm around the shoulder.

9. *Discipline with love.* Children need and want boundaries that tell them what is acceptable behavior and what isn't. Keep expectations clear. Limits that are set and then abandoned or moved capriciously are worse than no limits. Be fair, calm, consistent, evenhanded, predictable, and compassionate. Disciplining without spanking and yelling is crucially important. A technique that is much more effective than harsh scolding is catching your child doing something right and commending her for it, instead of constantly telling her when she has done something wrong.

10. *Listen to your child's ideas.* A child whose parents listen actively to her ideas, worries, issues, and problems, without judging or giving advice, is blessed many times over. Many parents don't do this, preferring to talk and be listened to, or listening only half-heartedly. Don't make that mistake. The more you listen to your child's ideas, the more confident she will become and the more likely she will be able to speak up and have her voice heard in life. Politeness and "good" behavior are desirable up to a point but, if you're not careful, this can quickly turn into submissiveness. Other people will be able to treat your child like a doormat, and no one wants that. She must refuse to be silenced.

11. *Get to know your child's friends.* Friends are a crucially important part of your child's life. Make a point of getting to know them and their parents. If your child arrives home upset because of difficulties with a friend, knowing the parents can help. It might be useful to call the parents of the friend to find out what is going on. Making an effort to get to know your child's friends and their parents sends a signal to your child that friendships are important.

12. *Get involved in your child's hobbies and interests.* Learn about his interests, whether they include soccer, ballet, chess, hip-hop, drawing, kickboxing, physics, World War II, or whatever else may spark his curiosity. Encourage his involvement in these areas and do whatever you can to be supportive.

13. *Help your child with her homework.* Don't do her homework for her, but be a constant and supportive presence—available to answer questions, offer encouragement, and advise as needed.

14. *Keep your promises to your child, and earn his trust.* Nothing builds trust between a child and his parents more quickly and firmly than keeping and fulfilling promises. If you say you'll be home from the office by 5 p.m. to take him to the circus, make sure you do that. More generally, make constant deposits of trust in your child's life. Instead of belittling your child, be kind. Instead of holding grudges and resentments, forgive.

15. *Tell your child that she is beautiful.* Films, television, and the Internet relentlessly tell your daughter she has to be skinny and dress provocatively in order to be cool and popular. When you tell her she is beautiful, you are helping her to accept herself and be happy in her own skin. Of course you will emphasize that beauty is more than skin-deep and what really matters is who she is, not what she looks like. Don't tell her she is "pretty" to the exclusion of everything else. Also praise her for her achievements which have nothing to do with her appearance, whether in sports, academics, or how she defends an acquaintance against bullies at school. Stress the beauty of her character. As the late Jeffrey Zaslow wrote in the *Wall Street Journal*, "Reams of research show that girls who are close to their dads are less likely to be promiscuous, develop eating disorders, drop out of school, or commit suicide."[1] The same goes for boys.

16. *Write letters and notes to your child.* Show your love for your child by finding opportunities to write him notes and letters telling him how much you love him and how proud you are of him.

17. *Teach your children responsibility and the value of hard work, self-discipline, and self-control.* The best way to do this is by example. Give

priority to the family, make and fulfill promises, and work diligently. Endure tough times, like a job loss, with optimism and grit. You want your child to understand her emotions so that, rather than suppressing them, she can use healthy and constructive methods to deal with sadness, fear, anger, and resentment. You want her to live with joy and purpose and with a zest for life. The corollary is to not to squander time on mindless pursuits like watching soap operas on television.

18. *Give your children chores to do around the house.* One way to prevent your child from becoming entitled, supercilious, and ungrateful is to give him a fair and reasonable number of chores to do to help the household run smoothly. He will enjoy contributing and rather than constantly taking and being waited on.

19. *Set high and clear expectations.* Effective and competent parents set high expectations for their kids (and for themselves, of course). They work with their children to achieve long-term goals and encourage them not to be afraid to make mistakes. A child learns from her mistakes, realizing that mistakes are a healthy and necessary part of the learning process and nothing to be embarrassed about. Parent and child celebrate when her goals are reached. Never tell her falsehoods or erroneous rationalizations, such as the myth that girls aren't good at math or engineering.

20. *Love your children unconditionally and express love frequently.* A parent who relates well to his child will express his love in a variety of meaningful ways. He finds lots of ways to express love every day, including saying, "I love you" and "I'm sorry." A key way to express love is through play—the language of children. Life must not only be chores, duties, and work. Having fun and lots of laughs is essential. Some fun is pure fun (hide and seek), while other types of fun (Scrabble) can have the purpose of teaching something. Play and teaching often go hand in hand.

21. *For girls, don't encourage the princess culture.* The princess culture, for the most part, encourages a girl to believe that her value comes from being attached to a man and that she will live happily ever after if she looks pretty and waits for a handsome prince to rescue her from troubles and distress. This is *not* something we want our daughters to learn!

22. *Protect your children from a toxic culture and from bullies.* Parents have an important role to play in protecting their children from sick and noxious material on the Internet and graphic violence in films. They have an equally important responsibility to equip their children to deal effectively with both bullying and cyberbullying. Many people are scarred for life by the cruelties and violence inflicted on them as children. I discuss this topic more in chapter 16.

23. *Help your children face their fears.* A parent can help a child get out of his comfort zone, try new things even though they are scary, and overcome his fears with courage. If a child avoids things that he fears, he won't have the opportunity to gain confidence in his ability to deal with stressful and scary situations.

24. *Don't be afraid to let your children feel uncomfortable.* Parents make a mistake when they rush in to save their children from every bit of discomfort. Let them struggle; in the struggle, they are learning. If you save your child every time, you are teaching her that she is helpless and weak. Whenever possible, let your child meet her own challenges, whether that means solving an algebra problem, writing a college essay, or resolving a disagreement with a friend. You want her to have courage and grit when faced with difficulties.

25. *Make feeling grateful an important family goal.* Help your children list in a simple notebook on a regular basis all the things for which they are grateful. This is a wonderful antidote to low moods and self-absorption. It will give your children a sharpened appreciation for how lucky they are, even when they run into a string of bad luck.

Don't underestimate your importance. A child needs to feel loved and secure to help her thrive in school and beyond. Being emotionally present and following the aforementioned "best practices" will help build a strong foundation for your child's success.

Kids with committed parents can sometimes forget how much their moms and dads sacrifice for them. But your sacrifice—if that is the right word for living more purposefully and for something larger than yourself—is totally overshadowed by the rewards of being a good parent.

JARED BECK

When I was growing up, my mother worked long hours as a nurse and she was the sole provider for the family, because my father was a disabled veteran. Neither of my parents went to college, and they married fresh out of high school.

Times were especially hard during the years when they were divorced. It felt like my mother was always at work or crying about missing an important event in my sister's or my life at school.

Because of these hardships, both my mother and my father put a huge emphasis on the importance of education for their children. I can remember from the very start of elementary school when they would tell me to do well in school so that I could get a scholarship to go to college.

Right before I entered high school, things began to change. My parents actually remarried, and my mother decided to enroll in college at the age of 40. She went on to earn not only a bachelor's degree, but master's and doctoral degrees as well. The timing of her pursuit of higher education was particularly appropriate, as it occurred when my sister and I began to worry about SAT scores and college applications. My mother became an exemplary model of pursuing higher education regardless of age, and heavily influenced my path to success in school. The academic and career achievements that I've made couldn't have been done without her guidance. My sister has earned two bachelor's degrees and is currently applying to medical school. As someone about to graduate with my own bachelor's degree and enter "the real world," I look forward to the future knowing that my mother will always have my back, no matter what.

Raising a child brings profound meaning to your life and a deep appreciation for the benefits of parenting. Overall, you will feel an intense joy and pride and an unmatched connection with the world. To give love is to give life, and to give life is to find purpose and meaning and to give your own life content and substance. As Jennifer Senior writes in her book *All Joy and No Fun*, "Children give structure, purpose, and stronger bonds to the world around us."[2]

This chapter has dealt with the fundamentals of being an effective, proactive, and vibrant parent. One way to start this process is to create a family mission statement. That is the focus of the next chapter.

KATIE BRYDEN

My father has always trusted my choices in school. So when I decided to be an environmental filmmaker and not take a more conventional path such as the one he took in earning an MBA, he never worried. He understood that I am hard working and determined, just like him. When I would come home from college for visits, I would share with him the many interesting topics I had learned about. We would get caught up in conversations about GMOs, carbon footprints, geo-engineering, and the like. He would always question the facts I was quoting and say, "Well that's not what I read." He would send articles to me at school and I would send articles back, trying my best to prove my point. But it was his skepticism that really pushed me to learn more and succeed in my field. It was those difficult questions and doing the extra research to respond that made me excel beyond the classroom.

Chapter 2

Create a Family Mission Statement

Creating a family mission statement is an opportunity to define vividly what your family stands for and the kind of family you want to have. The mission statement is a clear and compelling shared vision of your family at its best, with every member of the family thriving. It is the family's constitution or governing document, and it helps your family live to its fullest potential.

Sadly, in many families there is no vision of the family's purpose and meaning. It takes initiative, planning, and leadership to create a strong, shared vision. Parenting expert Meghan Leahy writes, "Parents know that if they don't create a value system for their family, our society will, and, frankly, we don't want society raising our children."[1]

JIM BULLARD

When I was in elementary school, my father drove me to school on his way to work as an executive at Kodak. Roadwork was being done along our route and I felt sorry for the men digging ditches in the bitter winter cold. My father asked me, rhetorically, "What's the difference between those men and your father?" He then answered, "They didn't work hard in school and they didn't go to college. I did, so I work in a warm office. It's your choice what kind of a life you want to live, and you'll be making that choice at school today." For months he asked the same question as we drove to school, and it made a huge impression on me.

In his book *The Seven Habits of Highly Effective Families*, Stephen R. Covey defines a family mission statement as "a combined, unified expression from all family members of what your family is all about—what it is you really want to do and be—and the principles you choose to govern your family life."[2]

Your family mission statement should focus on issues of enduring value and importance that help create a family in which everyone feels affirmed, loved, and appreciated. It should help all family members live fulfilled, productive, and purposeful lives that contribute, for example, to making the world a better place.

A mission statement will unify and strengthen your family and have a profound influence on how you go about living your daily lives together. It will help create a family with members who love, respect, and care for each other, who have fun together, grow together, learn together, and enjoy rich, meaningful relationships with each other.

Families should create a mission statement by the time the oldest child is about six years old, and then revisit it every year or so to update it and check to see if the family is on track.

In order to make such a statement work effectively, everyone in your family must contribute to its creation. Start by asking each family member the following questions:

1. What are the collective goals of our family?

2. What kind of a family do we want?

3. What kind of a home do we want to invite friends to?

4. What makes us want to come home?

5. How do we want to relate to one another?

6. What are the things that are truly important to us as a family?

7. What are our strengths and abilities?

8. What are our values? Kindness? Trust? Honesty? Empathy? Diligence? Fortitude? Unselfishness? Courage? Self-discipline? Compassion? Responsibility?

9. How do we want to make a difference in our community and to the world?

When everyone in the family has written answers to these questions, collect them and ask one member of the family (usually a mom or dad) to use the collective responses to formulate a series of declarations that will become the first draft of the family mission statement. Ask everyone in the family to review it and give feedback and comments. Absorb that feedback into a new draft. Edit it, polish it, and then post it in a location where everyone can see it on a daily basis.

ALICIA BURGESS

One of the most fundamental things my dad did to help me thrive in school was to provide a secure home environment. As the primary earner for my family, the roof over my head and the food on my plate were directly related to my dad's hard work and dedication. This stability was a key factor in giving me a stress-free childhood, and one that allowed me to focus my attention on school and homework.

It is important to make the family discussions around this topic fun, relaxed, and leisurely. Rushing the process, or having one person (e.g., the dad) do all the work, will quickly kill off any enthusiasm for creating a family mission statement, and eradicate any interest among family members in having "ownership" of it.

Stephen Covey loved to tell the story of the miracle of the Chinese bamboo tree. After the seed for this amazing tree is planted, you keep watering it day in and day out, but for five years see nothing. During those five years, all the growth is underground in a massive root structure that spreads deep and wide in the earth. Then, in the sixth year, the Chinese bamboo tree undergoes explosive growth and a trunk rises out of the ground to eighty feet!

ALICIA BURGESS

My dad usually introduced some form of competition into whatever we were doing (probably because he was a college athlete). One example is a tradition we had when our family went out to dinner together. My dad would quiz my brother and me while we waited for the food to arrive. He usually did multiplication tables, shouting "six times eight!" or "three times seven!" It was a race to see who could figure it out in his head and answer the fastest. My younger brother is much better at math than I, so getting the answer faster than he did was difficult. But I was always willing to fight for my pride.

Over the years, our learning through competition took different iterations. Playing along with "Jeopardy," completing crossword puzzles that had been clipped from the newspaper and floated around the house, or, now that we're older, playing trivia at the local bar, my dad always found a way to make learning fun. Not only did it help me pass third grade by mastering my times tables, it brought me an appreciation for learning that I carry with me today.

Covey pointed out that many things in family life are like the Chinese bamboo tree. You work and invest time and effort day after day, doing everything you can to nurture family members' growth and help them flourish. However, sometimes the results of your devotion and dedication aren't apparent.

But if you are patient, keep at it, and don't give up, then in that "sixth year" you will be astonished by what you have accomplished. A family mission statement that is vibrant, alive, and "owned" by every member of the family will help the family to reach that "sixth year" abundance, demonstrated, for example, by the high level of trust and love among family members.

Conversations about virtue and morality are far too scarce in families. Undertaking the creation of a family mission statement is one way to stress the importance of such values and to give your children some insight into what principles you believe are important for your family.

When your child is asked by someone (or he asks himself), "What is the meaning of life? What is its purpose?" he will be able to make a stab at answering those questions because he went through the process of creating a family mission statement. At least he will have the basis for answers. Preparing a family mission statement is one way to help your child begin to engage in issues of principles and values.

ALEXANDRA BENNETT CANNADY

Growing up in New York, my parents and uncle showed me our home through tourists' eyes. History came to life during family field trips to see the Statue of Liberty, Ellis Island, and New York's museums.

One year my Uncle Ray drove my aunt, mom, four cousins, and me from Dothan, Alabama, to St. Petersburg, Florida. He made a detour a couple of hours out of our way, not a good scene for three adults and five kids cramped in a station wagon.

When we arrived at his destination, he pointed to a statue erected to honor the boll weevil. He explained that if the insects had not destroyed cotton crops, farmers wouldn't have diversified. My cousins and I just shook our heads. We may not have appreciated it then, but my gratitude for my parents and uncle has grown and come full circle.

On my way home this past Thanksgiving, I took a detour to Tucka-hoe, Maryland, to show my five-year-old son the birthplace of Fred-erick Douglass. He's been to the Capitol, The White House, and the Udvar-Hazy Center of the Smithsonian Air and Space Museum. By the time he was three, he had started reading and could name the planets and the presidents.

I want to instill curiosity in him, as my uncle did for me. I hope it will propel him forward and also will take him back to see where his-tory was made.

You want your child to be not only highly capable and accomplished, but also equipped with moral purpose. You want him to be a good and moral person and know the difference between right and wrong.

You want him to be able to distinguish the difference between "resume virtues" and "eulogy virtues," concepts that David Brooks wrote about in 2015 in the *New York Times* to distinguish values we care about in order to advance our careers versus those we care about because we want to have a more meaningful life.[3]

In a similar vein, Leonard Sax writes in *The Collapse of Parenting*, "If you do not undertake this task [of stressing the importance of values] explicitly and seriously, and you happen to live in the United States today, then it is likely that your children will adopt the values of American popular culture, in which what matters most is the pursuit of fame, wealth, and good looks."[4]

Echoing Sax, Dr. Catherine Steiner-Adair writes in *The Big Disconnect*, "Fame is the do-it-yourself dream of the digital era. We're all indie artists eager for an audience on YouTube or streaming videos to viral success through social networks, so it is hardly surprising that fame is the number one value of adolescence and young adults."[5]

How does your child pursue a decent and moral life when the culture she is born into shows an absence of interest in that topic, and indeed in large part is an assault on such values because of its focus on violence, misogyny, and commercialism?

It's hard to be morally grounded and have a good character when you're surrounded by a cacophony of films, music, and video games that breach and violate boundaries of decency on a regular basis. If nothing else, all the noise and clutter militates against your child finding the time to reflect quietly on what deeply matters to her.

Your child needs a moral mentor, and her parents are the obvious can-didates. Creating a family mission statement is a fruitful task to undertake in your role as a moral mentor for your child. Her mind will become more attuned to the responsibilities of citizenship, how to enhance the public good, and the importance of social responsibility.

NELSON COONEY

Mother was my lifeline for early learning in our family. Father wasn't too involved. It was because of her that I took piano lessons and played duets with her when she played the violin. Other cultural pursuits included visits to museums, art galleries, and concerts. To nurture reading she would walk us little tots the two miles to the public library for story hour every Wednesday. Even in sports, it was she who took my brother and me on the bus to swimming lessons in summer at the public pools, and to an ice skating rink in winter to learn skating and ice hockey. She also took us to boxing lessons and dancing school.

Fortunately for us, mother was a tomboy at heart and an early feminist, gaining a foothold in a man's world by administering anesthesia in the operating room. After marriage, she accepted the traditional role of at-home mom, and devoted herself to providing opportunities for her two sons.

Writing a family mission statement will create a foundation for your family life that will help your child thrive in school. It will help to teach your child sound values, including those values especially important for achieving success in school and in growing up to be a successful adult, such as empathy, diligence, tenacity, curiosity, resilience, self-control, perseverance, and fortitude.

Having composed a family mission statement, the next task is to create an approach to life for your family that is rich in fun, vibrancy, and life-affirming traditions. That is the topic of the next chapter.

Chapter 3

Create Family Traditions and Rituals

According to child-rearing expert Dr. Ron Taffel, kids today are suffering from very high levels of chronic anxiety and worry. A major reason for this anxiety, he argues in his book *The Second Family: How Adolescent Power Is Changing the American Family*, is that "there is less adult presence in our children's lives." Parents have frenetic and intense lives, he says, and are simply not available enough to their children.[1]

To fill this parental vacuum, kids are lured into the world of pop culture and close relationships with their peers, what Taffel calls "the second family." He writes, "Today, the first family doesn't have the same gravitational pull as the second family. Kids are with each other every day and provide each other with much needed comfort time."

Taffel is concerned that parents don't really understand the relentless barrage of messages their children are absorbing online and from movies, music, and television. Many of these messages are negative, brutal, hateful, misogynistic, and terrifying. He says that most children are not emotionally ready to deal with them, and that this contributes to their worry and anxiety.

ANNA CUMMINS

When I look back on my love for school as a child and then beyond, I can pinpoint a few exceptional things my parents did to inspire my love of learning. The first is one I can only tell stories about. The second I can emulate, now that I am the parent of a four-year-old girl. And the third and most important one simply has to be lived.

First: My father created the school that I attended. It was a school called Crossroads, in Santa Monica, California. It was built upon the philosophy that kids are unique learners and beings, all with their own way of expressing themselves, and making their own contribution to the world. Early on, he met my musician mother, one of the most passionate teachers he'd ever met. Our household was a revolving door of teachers, parents, alumni, visitors, mentors, and more. Family dinner was a staple, guests were the norm, and my younger sister and I were encouraged to participate. My home life and my school life were inextricably linked.

Second: From day one, my parents lavished us with their love of books, literature, and writing. Both of them read to my sister and me every night. My father took us to secondhand bookstores or the library to spend leisurely Saturday afternoons treasure hunting. I became a bookworm, building secret forts to hide away with a stack of books and a flashlight. And though I had extracurricular activities—violin lessons and sports (softball, fencing)—I also had plenty of unstructured time to read, wander, daydream, and just to be.

Third: My parents model their belief in pursuing passion and meaning in work. They both love their work wholeheartedly, and are dedicated to education, community, and justice. My father has always been an admirer of the poet Robert Frost. I remember him sharing these lines when I was young, and explaining their meaning:

"My goal in life is to unite my avocation with my vocation, as my two eyes make one in sight."

And while I realize today that this is a blessing, that not everyone has the fortune or the luxury to pursue meaningful work; this left an indelible impression on me. I was always encouraged to follow my heart, a path that led me to pursue sustainability—and also to pursue learning for my own sake.

Dr. Leonard Sax makes a similar point in his excellent book *The Collapse of Parenting*. He writes, "We now live in a culture in which kids value the opinion of same-age peers more than they value the opinions of their parents. . . . The authority of parents, and even more significantly, the *importance* of parents, in the lives of their children has declined substantially."[2]

One of the most effective ways to prevent your child from drifting away into the relentless and saturnine world of pop culture and peer pressure is to remain present in her life. There is nothing quite like a strong, caring, and devoted parent to give a child the strength to deal with all the anxiety and pressure the world imposes on her.

But remaining present in your child's life is not easy, especially as he gets older and wants to be distinct and differentiated from his parents. Creating family traditions and rituals is one important way in which parents can stay connected to their kids, remain important and relevant to them, and create happy childhood memories for the entire family.

Family traditions bring predictability, structure, stability, comfort, and fun that help your child feel secure in a world that otherwise can often feel very insecure and dangerous. Treasured traditions and rituals can come to mean a great deal to him.

Many family rituals revolve around holidays, such as Thanksgiving, Halloween, and St. Patrick's Day. They may incorporate watching a favorite family movie or decorating the house in a particular way. Other family rituals involve meals, bedtimes, weekends, or birthdays. Some rituals can be simple, such as reading a book aloud before bedtime every night. They don't have to be fancy, expensive, or elaborate.

As your child grows older, you may find it tempting to give up on family rituals. The life of your child, and of all family members, is busy and schedules are jammed. Family together time can get pretty thin and fleeting, but don't drop family rituals.

Remember that the rituals in your child's "second family" are powerful. She and her friends text on their phones all the time and share in whatever's trending. They meet every weekend, they watch the same streamed Internet programs, and they play the same video games simultaneously. The competition for your child's time is strong, so family traditions and rituals must be strong as well.

MIKE DANTE

What my mother gave me was the confidence that I could do what I hadn't done before. To set the stage, during the Depression my father worked twelve- or fourteen-hour days. With several small children, my mother was basically overwhelmed. Before I was old enough to go to school, she called upon me, the eldest of her kids, to help her.

I remember helping her change the babies' diapers. This was back in the days before Pampers so it was necessary to hold a wiggling child while fastening a folded cloth diaper with safety pins, without stabbing the baby. I also served as a babysitter, and helped with cooking, doing more and more the older I got. Helping with cooking continued until I could actually cook on my own. This was a valuable skill to have once I left home.

I also remember getting things from the grocery store. My mother started by sending me up to the corner store with exact change so I could buy what she had shown me to buy. But by the time I was in school, I was able to go to the Safeway, which involved crossing a major street.

Thinking back, I know that my mother gave me the self-confidence to do adult tasks even before I started school. This is a lesson that I think all children ought to be taught. They should learn that there is no limit to what they can do if they try, and that with minimal direction they can learn how to do things if they keep at it.

What follows are four suggested traditions and rituals that are worth making part of your family's DNA.

1. HAVE DINNER TOGETHER

Studies show that when families make it a habit to eat together, kids are less likely to have high stress or indulge in risky behaviors. Family dinner time creates an opportunity for discussion and for sharing ideas.

Consider serving dinner in courses, so the meal is less rushed and there's more time to talk. And don't stop at traditional dinners. Have occasional picnics and Sunday brunches.

Come up with conversation topics and issues to raise for discussion. Ask everyone to talk about her "roses" and "thorns" for the day—that is, what went well and what didn't go so well. By watching others, including her parents, navigate ups and downs, a child learns how to do the same, and also develops empathy with those around her.

Overall, the goal is to have family dinner conversations, in which there is a sense of gratitude, appreciation, joy, bonding, hope, optimism, acceptance, and serenity—as opposed to conversations that are inhibited, moody, resentful, uncomfortable, distracted, and tense.

2. HOLD FAMILY MEETINGS

As Don Dinkmeyer and Gary McKay explain in their book *The Parent's Handbook*, the family meeting is a regularly scheduled gathering, usually once a week, of all family members to make plans for family fun and family chores, to encourage each other, to air complaints and grievances, to resolve conflicts, to express concerns and worries, and to make decisions.[3]

It is an important opportunity to recognize the good things happening in the family, encourage all members for the efforts they are making, and plan family vacations (don't just focus on complaints and conflicts).

Using family meetings to plan for fun things to do as a family is particularly important. Parenting expert Meghan Leahy writes, "Whether [the children] are introverts, extroverts, sporty, artsy, silly or serious, effective parents recognize play as key to development."[4]

Meet at the same time each week, have a written agenda, let everyone be heard, and treat all family members as equals. Agree on the start time and length of the meeting, start and finish on time, record the commitments that family members make, and post those commitments where everyone can be reminded of them.

Start each meeting by going over the commitments from the last family meeting to see if family members have kept their promises and followed through. It is important that no one person dominates the meeting, and that everyone takes a turn to chair the meeting and create the agenda.

3. KEEP A FAMILY JOURNAL

For the first few years of your child's life, mothers have a crucial role and fathers have a supportive role. Both are important. One way for a father to increase his importance and produce something that will become a family heirloom is to keep a family journal.

This is a way for a father to express his love and devotion to his family, to bridge the distance between himself and his child, and to create a close bond with him. The journal can describe the details of daily life, including the joys and the disappointments, as well as the feelings the father has about being the child's parent.

In some families, it will be valuable for a mother to write a family journal. Some mothers may not be good communicators, and some may be single parents.

Parents are likely to have thoughts that they can't easily talk about with their family, but are willing to put down on paper. A family journal will help a parent get in touch with his feelings about being a parent. It also will become a testament to his desire for a close and loving relationship with his child.

4. WRITE LETTERS AND NOTES

Writing "love letters" to your child is a family tradition rich with positive long-term consequences. It is a chance to compliment your child, affirm him, tell him how he has enriched your life and how much he means to you, thank him, give him encouragement, and tell him you love him.

If you travel away from home on business, leaving a letter for every night you are away is a very special gift to your child. You can use email, FaceTime, text messaging, and so on, to stay connected, but the quick and fleeting nature of such communications has led to the demise of the thoughtful, reflective letter. This is a loss, because writing letters is one way to strengthen the bond between parents and kids that can be frayed and weakened by busyness.

In a 1983 column in the *Washington Post*, Maureen Dowd told the moving story of how her relationship with her mother, once strained and stilted, was transformed when her mother started to write letters to her, and especially as the letters became more intimate. Dowd's mother could say things in letters that she couldn't say on the phone or in person.[5]

Many parents are like that. They are not good at expressing their feelings in person. Their children don't realize how much their parents love them and are proud of them. Because they don't express their feelings, some parents, especially dads, become emotionally distant from their kids. This deprives their children of parental love and nurturing. It can result in long-term damage to kids, such as ingrained feelings of inadequacy.

Writing expressive letters or notes—leaving them in her lunch box, under her pillow, in her backpack, taped to the steering wheel, wherever—can go a long way toward strengthening your bond with your child.

Parents need to take a leadership role in helping the family spend time together. It may mean not letting your kids drift to their "second family" because of busy schedules, and not allowing competing attractions, such as a television show, to interrupt family plans.

Protect family traditions and rituals. They give you and your kids a chance to bond. They give your family members a chance to share their lives, to connect, to communicate, and to listen. They give your child a positive grounding that will help him do well in many of life's endeavors.

SUJAY DAVÉ

My parents helped me thrive academically in many ways, but I think the things that had the biggest impact were the sky-high expectations and an instilled love for reading.

The value of education was almost a mantra in my house. The importance of doing well in school was constantly reinforced and my mom, in particular, always made sure I had a never-ending supply of enrichment activities, extra problems, and workbooks. I was encouraged to try hard and enjoy learning. My family also viewed reading as a hobby, so I quickly developed a ravenous appetite for books. That led to a virtuous cycle of academic success.

Even more important than family traditions and rituals is modeling positive behavior as a person. That is the topic of the next chapter.

Chapter 4

Model Good Behavior

Your kids are always watching what you do. They see how you treat other people, how you handle disappointments, and how you express your feelings. They observe your language. They watch your manners. They follow your media consumption. They catch onto your demeanor.

Children are highly observant, and soak up everything about the most important people in their lives—their parents. That is why the most important parenting skill you can have is setting a good example and being a positive role model.

ADITI DESAI

It was a big day. *The* day. After weeks of riding my new bike with training wheels, my dad was going to pull them off. I would be on my own. I was terrified. Could I do it? Was I strong enough, balanced enough, smart enough? The fears ate at me until my seven-year-old self was shaking with worry.

My dad unscrewed the wheels and it was time. He held onto my seat as I pedaled my sweet purple ride. My absolute favorite color. My dad kept me on course, running alongside me. Fear left my body and was replaced by joy. The wind kissed my face and whooshed by my ears.

"Keep going, keep going," my dad encouraged, with much laughter. I quickly looked back and realized he had let go. I was alone. For a split second, I hesitated. My bike wobbled as the fear crept back. "Just keep going," he shouted, with a broad smile on his face. And I did.

That encouragement propelled me from elementary school through graduate school. Regardless of fear, I never balked at a challenge. "Keep going" was my mantra. I moved to India for school and work. I took flying lessons. I pursued my passion for storytelling. Learning to ride a bike with my dad by my side on that sunny afternoon so many years ago gave me the courage to do so much more. I kept going.

Your kids will learn from watching how you act, whether the example you set is good or bad.

You are asking for trouble if you:

- Smoke cigarettes, but tell your child never to smoke;

- Eat ice cream surreptitiously after your child goes to bed, but tell him not to eat ice cream because it's full of sugar;

- Rarely exercise, but tell your child she ought to work out more;

- Snap at a waitress for bringing the wrong food order, but tell your child to be kind and respectful to others;

- Watch television every evening, but tell your child he needs to watch less television and read more;

- Lash out verbally at another driver when he cuts in front of you, but tell your child not to lose her temper;

- Tell a friend you can't help her for some fictitious reason, but tell your child never to lie.

If you want your child to know right from wrong, to have good morals, to live by the golden rule, and to have empathy for others, then it is crucial that you, her parents, be moral people who behave kindly, decently, and with integrity.

In *The Collapse of Parenting*, Dr. Leonard Sax writes, "There is one inescapable truth: *you must teach by example.* You can't expect your child to exercise self-control if you stay up past midnight watching TV or surfing on the web. You can't expect your child to be responsible if you don't keep your word. . . . To become a better parent, you must become a better person."[1]

Jennifer Senior makes a similar point in *All Joy and No Fun*. She writes, "The most productive, generative adults see their children as their superegos. . . . Their kids hover over them and guide all of their moral choices. If these adults falter or behave ignobly, they know their kids will see; the same is true if they do well. They are exquisitely aware of themselves as role models. They know they are being watched."[2]

SUSAN DEVICO

My dad, a first-generation American, the son of a lamplighter and a seamstress, took our education *very* seriously.

He was the first in his family to graduate from college, attending NYU (at night). He edited the student newspaper, while working hard at his day job.

A conscientious parent, he was keen for us to excel academically. He always encouraged us to be aware of current events and politics, and to expand our knowledge of history. All manner of newspapers and magazines were available in the house. We were actively encouraged to read and discuss them. As a family, we watched a great deal of television news programs as well.

I believe the wealth of journalistic resources made available to us as youngsters contributed mightily to our being well-informed citizens, conversant in current events, who can form and clearly articulate an informed point of view.

All of this likely had a great deal to do with my winding up working in network news and, later, environmental advocacy.

Here are nine things you can do to be a good role model for your children.

1. TAKE CARE OF YOURSELF

It is nearly impossible to take care of others if you do not take care of yourself. Don't ignore your own needs. If you do, you will not have the capacity and capability to meet the needs of your child. You need to bring your best self to your responsibilities as a parent.

Do things for your own well-being, such as journaling, meditation, yoga, jogging, and joining a parent support group. Say "no" to unimportant activities, so you have the time for what *is* important.

Take care of yourself physically, mentally, emotionally, and spiritually. Role modeling good health in all of these areas can inspire your child to do the same. Get regular daily exercise and plenty of sleep, eat nutritious meals, get regular checkups. Commit yourself to constant learning. Maintain comfortable stress levels. Spend time with friends and loved ones. Imbue your life with meaning and purpose. These are behaviors and activities that shape a positive role model for your child.

Parenting expert Meghan Leahy writes, "Effective parents place their own needs high on their list of priorities. When these needs are met, the parents feel fulfilled. And when parents feel fulfilled, they can calmly turn to their family with renewed energy, feeling deeply grounded and ready for whatever comes their way. Balanced parents create balance in their families."[3]

2. CREATE A PERSONAL MISSION STATEMENT

Create a personal mission statement in which you describe what matters most to you and what kind of parent, spouse, and person you want to be. Make personal development and lifelong learning a high priority. This is in addition to the family mission statement discussed in chapter 2. Both documents should resonate with each other and be consistent.

Live morally, ethically, conscientiously, and with intention. Be reliable and trustworthy, work hard, be curious, and have a sense of humor. Follow through on commitments and keep promises, so the trust between you and your child grows and strengthens.

3. SHOW THAT ADULT LIFE IS ENJOYABLE

By the way you live your life, show your child that life is enjoyable. Give your child something to look forward to, so she wants to grow up. When a child sees her parents stressed, unhappy, overwhelmed, and tense, it doesn't give her much incentive to become an adult. If being an adult is relentless misery, what is the point of growing up?

One of the greatest gifts you can give your child is showing that there is something in your life that gives you profound joy and vibrancy. Show her that you have achieved a work/life balance that brings joy and happiness to yourself and to your whole family.

4. GET OUT OF YOUR COMFORT ZONE

Don't be complacent or settle for second best. Be bold and take prudent risks. You want your child to see you taking risks in life in order to gain rewards.

If you want to improve your life, then you have to stop doing the same things over and over. To get closer to your goals, you have to experience the discomfort of change. Show your child that you have the confidence to take risks and make yourself vulnerable to discomfort and disappointment in an effort to move forward.

5. BE GRATEFUL

Make a list of what you are grateful for and share it with your kids. Thank them when they do something helpful. Thank others too, such as a waitress in a restaurant or a clerk in a store. Your child needs to see you expressing gratitude in a sincere and meaningful way.

Try not to take for granted little acts of service from others, including your kids. Instead, notice and express appreciation for them.

Throughout the day, mentally note the things that make your life a pleasure and that you might take for granted, such as the blue sky, majestic trees, running water, clean clothes, the love of your family, and living in a democratic society.

Share your thoughts with your children and show them how you count your blessings. Keep a gratitude journal or joy list (relationships, projects, experiences, and feelings that you are grateful for) and encourage your kids to do the same.

Demonstrate gratitude to your family and other people in your life. Author and political commentator E. J. Dionne Jr. writes, "A genuine sense of gratitude is rooted in the realization that when I think about all that I am, all that I have, and all that I might have achieved, I cannot claim to have done any of this by myself. None of us is really 'self-made.' We must all acknowledge the importance of the help, advice, comfort, and loyalty that came from others."[4]

6. TRY NOT TO BE MATERIALISTIC

Show that your life is more than your possessions. Try not to attach excessive importance to materialism, acquisitions, and consumerism. Show your children that your interest is in service and experiences rather than in material goods. For example, think about volunteering at a nursing home or homeless shelter and inviting your son to join you.

It's hard not to be materialistic when we see advertisements everywhere. Corporations even reach out with advertisements directly to children, hoping they will pester their parents to buy them things they don't really need.

This is another reason to minimize television at home. In her book *The Shelter of Each Other*, Dr. Mary Pipher describes the not-so-hidden messages in advertisements. They include the idea that buying things is important; the concept that "I want what I want now and I am the center of the universe"; the sense that "I am unhappy with what I have now"; and the suggestion that material things will bring happiness. These messages help to create an ugly sense of entitlement in a child.[5]

But obviously we all do need to buy things. In her book *Smart Mom, Rich Mom: How to Build Wealth While Raising a Family*, personal finance author Kimberly Palmer writes about the importance of having discussions with your child on the topics of saving money and planning purchases. She suggests having talks about money with your kids early so that they understand how finances work. This might mean balancing your checkbook with them so they understand why you made certain purchases.[6] (Full disclosure: Kimberly Palmer is my daughter.)

7. SHOW THAT ADVERSITY IS A GIFT

Show your child how you deal responsibly with stress, mistakes, and setbacks in your life. Show that adversity can be a gift and that mistakes can be our best teachers. We need to learn from them and become more capable because of them.

Failing does not mean a person is a failure. Failing has a stigma it doesn't deserve. Yes, failing is unpleasant, but it is an essential part of striving and learning. When you take the necessary precursors to success—trying hard and taking risks—failing is bound to happen sometimes.

If a person is not failing, then he is unlikely to be on the path to advance toward ultimate success. The best way for a child to acquire this wisdom is to see it embodied in the way his parents live their lives.

8. CAREFULLY SELECT THE MEDIA YOU VIEW

Set a good example by selecting carefully and judiciously your information sources. Refer to reliable sources rather than inflammatory or fake news sources.

If you see an ad, product, or program that objectifies or belittles women (or others) or portrays them negatively, talk about it with your children. Write a letter together to the company responsible for the ad, product, or program, stating your objections to the harmful message. Ask that they stop conveying that message.

9. USE GOOD MANNERS

Teach your kids the desirability and benefits of good manners by using good manners yourself. Show them how to shake hands with people, look others in the eye, smile, and enter into a relaxed and amicable conversation.

SIRJAUT KAUR DHARIWAL

Growing up, my siblings and I were the only Sikh–Americans in our school district. Our differences were very apparent: our unshorn hair, our turbans (worn mainly by men), our unique names. These distinctions could have sullied our learning experience with ridicule and bullying, like what so many children endure.

Thankfully, our parents recognized that our classmates would be more understanding and open to diversity if they knew more about Sikhism. Our parents took the time out of their busy schedules to give our classes (and teachers) in-depth presentations about our religion. This broke barriers among our peers, creating a space where questions were encouraged. We learned to embrace our differences rather than using them as reasons for exclusion.

These presentations not only educated my classmates, but also instilled a sense of identity and pride within me at a very young age. I went through school with confidence, which allowed me to thrive academically and be sure of who I am. That confidence continues to shape my life now that I am an adult.

Table manners are important too. Good manners demonstrate respect for others at the table. Don't talk with your mouth full or chew with your mouth open. Don't use electronic devices at the table. Do help clean up after the meal is over.

When you teach your child good manners, you are giving her an important life skill. Judith Martin, better known as advice columnist "Miss Manners," says that "learning good manners is an essential part of childrearing."

* * *

This is the big challenge of being a parent—to be someone your children will love, respect, and admire. There is no higher calling than to be all we can be, so we can give it to our kids.

By modeling good behavior, parents help their children do well in school and in life, because kids learn from what their parents do, not what they say. You teach what you are.

But being a good role model will only take you so far as a parent. You also have to exert wise discipline and set limits. That is the topic of the next chapter.

Chapter 5

Exert Wise Discipline and Responsibility

The essence of effective parenting is to be extraordinarily loving while also being strict. By strict I don't mean authoritarian, dictatorial, or domineering. Rather, I mean not being permissive. Have standards of behavior to which you expect everyone in the family to adhere; set fair limits and boundaries; and enforce those limits fairly, consistently, and kindly.

Dr. Leonard Sax writes in his book *The Collapse of Parenting* that there are three types of parenting styles: authoritarian ("too hard"), permissive ("too soft"), and authoritative ("just right")[1]:

- "Too hard" parents believe that they should be in total control. They want to be obeyed, and they show little affection or kindness to their children. Harsh parents like this can verge on being abusive because they tend to be relentlessly critical of every perceived shortcoming.

- "Too soft" parents want to be their children's best friends and, while demonstrating love and affection, don't enforce any rules or boundaries.

- "Just right" parents make rules and set standards which they enforce consistently and with kindness. They also express abundant love for their kids. Sax writes that "just right" or authoritative parents "are strict, within reasonable bounds, *and* also loving."

The best parenting style, of course, is "just right," but Sax says many parents today are too permissive ("too soft") and don't have enough rules and limits. Good parents are not afraid to say such things as:

- "You can't watch your favorite TV show until you've eaten your vegetables"

- "You can't watch TV or go online or play video games until you've done your homework"

- "You have to do your chores before you use your cell phone"

- "You can't eat cotton candy because it's junk food"

- "You are not allowed to have a television in your room"

- "No electronic devices or TV are allowed during family dinners"

- "You can't watch a PG-13 movie because it contains inappropriate material"

- "We are having spinach, broccoli and tomatoes for lunch, not French fries"

This is not being too strict, especially if you calmly add a reasonable explanation or rationale. It is the essence of effective parenting to set reasonable limits in order to teach your children how to gain self-control and learn self-discipline.

Sax writes in *The Collapse of Parenting* that "a child's self-control at age 11 or 14 is a good predictor of the child's health and happiness 20 years later, when the child is in his or her 30s."[2]

Consequently, one main responsibility of parents is to teach their children self-control. Kids must learn that they can't necessarily have the latest extravagant digital gadget. Parents must teach children what is really important—values, such as honesty, hard work, kindness, generosity, and delayed gratification. Parents should not allow kids to be grasping, greedy, rude, selfish, or disrespectful. Over-indulged and acquisitive children grow up to be self-absorbed adults with a distorted sense of entitlement.

ERICA DOMINITZ

My parents taught my sister and me about the importance of learning for the sake of learning, as opposed to learning the bare minimum necessary to get by on a test. In other words, there are no shortcuts to learning. I will never forget the time that I was in third or fourth grade and my class was learning about simple machines, such as levers and pulleys. The night before my test on the subject, as I was putting away my notebook and heading to bed, my dad offered to go over the material with me to make sure that I was ready for my test. About five minutes into our study session, which I incorrectly had assumed would take no longer than ten minutes, my father realized that I did not really grasp how simple machines work or what purposes they served. (Apparently they were not so simple after all.)

To my great consternation, my dad reached into my schoolbag and pulled out my textbook so that he could review with me the *entire* chapter about simple machines (which must have been at least twenty pages long). I tried to explain to him that this comprehensive (translation: tedious and boring) review was completely unnecessary because all that my teacher expected us to do on the test was to look at pictures of different simple machines and write their names underneath. But this explanation did not satisfy my dad. Not even close.

We read the entire chapter together, and then talked through the concepts until my dad was satisfied that I knew not only the names, but also the functions and practical uses, of various simple machines. We were up until midnight. I was exhausted, cranky, and less than appreciative, but by the time we were done there was no doubt that I had really learned the subject matter. It was not until I was older that I appreciated the lesson that my dad taught me. It's a lesson that I am now trying to teach to my own children. Of course, they appreciate these lectures and torture sessions as much as I did when I was their age. But I am hopeful that, when they are older, they too will see the benefit and will pass this lesson along to their children.

The examples above of what "just right" parents say to their kids may give the impression that "just right" parenting is intrinsically downbeat, dour, and bleak. That is incorrect. "Just right" parents spend most of their time with their kids listening, loving, playing, laughing, talking, problem solving, hugging, reading, and praising, so their children feel treasured and special. "Just right" parents are highly effective, capable, and loving parents. What spoils a child is too few limits, not too much love.

Setting boundaries and limits, and establishing a home with order, structure, and schedules, helps children feel secure and safe. They recognize that they are in a nurturing environment where they can flourish and develop the "self-control muscles" so essential to achieving success in life. For example, creating a routine for after school encourages children to delegate their time sensibly to homework, chores, eating, and fun activities.

Setting limits means parents have to learn to say no. If parents fail this test, a child can become very unhappy and feel out of control. The child senses that she has too much power over her parents, and this can be terrifying to her. Children like parents to set rules because then they know what is expected of them. Rules reduce their anxiety and uncertainty. Boundaries also tell kids that they can't always get their way—and this helps them begin to understand how the real world works.

By enforcing rules, parents remind their children that they are ultimately in charge. This is what children want to hear. Parents should warmly encourage their children to share their opinions on family goals, projects, and activities. But parents should assert their authority to make the final decision, especially when kids are young. Setting limits consistently, firmly, and gently builds children's respect for their parents.

KAKKY DYE

My dad grew up in a time when women stayed at home to raise the children and men were busy with work. His own parents filled these roles. But my dad was different. He shared household chores with my mom and made us dinner when she worked late. He picked me up from school every day. He taught me how to ride my bike and drive a car. I had the kind of relationship with my dad that a lot of kids didn't experience growing up. I'm lucky my dad broke the traditional mold of parenting by simply helping my mom at home and spending time with us.

I never felt pressured to act like a stereotypical girl when I was growing up. Instead of wearing pink and hosting tea parties, my dad encouraged me to read and play street hockey with the neighborhood boys. He taught me the meaning of gender equality and that girls can achieve anything boys can. My dad didn't teach me this consciously or deliberately. He was simply letting me make my own choices without judgment.

When I was sixteen and in high school, I began dating. My father wasn't thrilled with this new idea, but accepted it. I dated someone outside my race, in a community where I knew it would be difficult. I had a family member ignore me for months and friends crack jokes at our expense. I was feeling sad and disappointed. My dad told me how proud he was of me for being who I am. His words gave me encouragement to face adversity and be true to myself.

I was not the best student in the classroom growing up. My dad, on the other hand, has always been a walking encyclopedia. He knows the name of every bird, the date for every historical event, and the origin of every word. He always has a book in his hand and never stops reading. I wanted to be smart like him but watched my grades gradually fall as years passed. I began listening to his high school stories, and I realized how similar we were. He struggled in school just like me. He was tenacious and resilient in his work in order to succeed. I learned from his actions how to dedicate myself to work harder than most and achieve more for myself. Now, I too always have a book in hand.

Sax writes in *The Collapse of Parenting* that, "Over the past three decades, there has been a massive transfer of authority from parents to kids. . . . What kids think and what kids like and what kids want now matters as much, or more, than what their parents think and like and want." Sax believes this change has been "profoundly harmful" to children[3] because kids cannot thrive when they perceive their parents to lack authority.

Parenting is an art, not a science, so determining how to set limits is a process of trial and error. You need to figure out what works best for your family and for your child's unique character and disposition.

Obviously, parenting styles will change as a child gets older. When a child is young, parents clearly have to be in charge. As she becomes a teenager and then a young adult, parents slowly relinquish that role and gradually encourage their child to govern and shape her own life.

In addition to setting limits and deluging your family with expressions of love, here are six ideas for balancing discipline and reinforcement of your child's behavior.

1. CATCH YOUR CHILDREN DOING SOMETHING RIGHT

Management guru Ken Blanchard once said, "People who feel good about themselves produce good results, and people who produce good results feel good about themselves." It's a virtuous cycle built on the concept of catching people doing something right and it applies to families as much as to organizations.[4]

One of the easiest and quickest ways parents can help their family succeed is to notice, encourage, and celebrate the good things that are happening and to take the time to intentionally focus on those good things. Too many parents make the error of only catching their kids making mistakes.

2. PRAISE SKILLFULLY AND ENCOURAGE GENEROUSLY

This notion is closely related to #1 above. All of us, but especially children, respond powerfully when praised and encouraged accurately and specifically for something good we have done. For example, "Joe, I really liked how you showed concern for your little sister yesterday when she was upset about losing her doll." Or "Sarah, yesterday morning when you came downstairs for breakfast, I noticed you gave Mom a lovely smile. I love to see that!" Or "Susan, thanks for remembering to feed the dog today." Or "Michael, I'm proud of you for sitting down to do your homework without any reminder from me."

Nagging, or offering endless and ill-natured reminders, is ineffective and makes you rather than your child take on the bulk of the responsibility. Instead, look for the slightest sign of the behavior you are seeking and praise it. Sadly, in some families good behavior often goes unnoticed. Praise and encouragement motivate children to keep doing the good things they are doing.

In *The Parent's Handbook*, Don Dinkmeyer and Gary McKay draw a distinction between praise and encouragement. They recommend focusing more on encouragement, "which is given for effort or improvement, however slight."[5] In contrast, praise is an attempt to motivate kids with external rewards. It involves comparing the child with others.

Encouragement builds feelings of adequacy, worthiness, and self-respect, and parents should be generous with encouragement. It attempts to motivate children through internal means. Examples include:

- "I appreciate you doing that"
- "I like the way you handled that problem"
- "You are improving"
- "You worked diligently on that essay"
- "You kept working on that math problem until you solved it"
- "You deserve to feel proud of the A grade you got"
- "I have confidence you can handle it"
- "You may not have reached your goal, but look how far you've come"

The Parent's Handbook argues that encouragement values kids as they are, points out the positive aspects of behavior, shows faith in kids so that they can come to believe in themselves, and recognizes effort and improvement, as well as accomplishments. But having said that, both praise and encouragement are important.

3. EMPLOY NATURAL CONSEQUENCES

Kids can be forgetful, careless, disorganized, and impulsive. One way to teach them responsibility is to let them experience the natural consequences of their behavior. The idea is that the negative consequences from mistakes are directly linked to the errant behavior—and are instructive to children. For example, if a child carelessly leaves his gloves at home, you might choose to let him endure cold hands rather than rushing to school with the gloves. Don't rescue your child from every discomfort; allow him to grow wiser from them.

4. EXPRESS ANGER RARELY, IF AT ALL,
AND DON'T OVERREACT

Most parents will occasionally feel angry with their kids and lose their temper. This is never acceptable because it exhibits the worst side of you—a frightening, out-of-control side—and also sets a bad example of not keeping your emotions under control. I don't want to pretend that I've always succeeded here. I've struggled with losing my temper like most parents.

If you react intemperately when your child accidentally spills milk all over the kitchen floor, then he will go to great lengths to avoid your bad temper in the future, probably including lying about future spills.

Harsh discipline, says discipline expert Amy Morin, "turns kids into good liars." She writes, "While it's important to discipline your child when he breaks the rules, don't be too tough on him. Keep the focus on teaching your child to take responsibility for his own behavior, rather than punishing him for his mistakes."[6]

5. NEVER SPANK, HIT, OR YELL

Spanking, hitting, and yelling don't work. They only hurt your child's self-worth, self-respect, and self-confidence. They also set a bad example, and teach kids that violence and anger are the way to deal with problems. The American Academy of Pediatrics (AAP) opposes spanking under any circumstances. Instead, AAP recommends time-outs, which typically involve denying the child any interaction for a specified period of time.[7]

Beyond their counterproductive nature, says parent coach Meghan Leahy, "spankings have been shown to cause anxiety and depression . . . and [serve] to hinder emotional growth and strength."[8]

Discipline is not about punishing kids for bad behavior. Rather it is about teaching them the life skills they need to become responsible and exercise self-control.

6. ASSIGN CHORES

Doing family chores builds character and reminds kids that life is not one long vacation. Chores teach self-discipline, teamwork, family loyalty, responsibility, competence, and familiarity with how the real world works. They teach children not to feel entitled and overly dependent on others. They are empowering.

Every family member contributes to running the house, so that everyone has food to eat, clean clothes to wear, and an organized home to live in.

A child learns that life has meaning beyond satisfying her own immediate needs. Chores help her feel good about herself.

Before you show disappointment and displeasure when your child doesn't do his chores properly, it may be wise to check that he has been taught how to do the job. "Clean your room" can mean something very different to a child and a parent. You may have to spend time showing the child exactly what you want and how you want it done. Show what responsible behavior looks like.

Parents should avoid sexism when assigning chores. Use gender neutral parenting to eliminate bias at home with regard to everything, including cooking, cleaning, and laundry.

It is best to do chores as a collective family activity. For example, when cleaning up after family dinner, everyone should help and no one should leave until the kitchen is clean and ready for breakfast the next morning.

*   *   *

As noted, one main responsibility of parents is to exert wise discipline and responsibility, so their children can learn self-control and self-discipline.

BAILEY EDELSTEIN

No price can be placed on a father's wisdom. My teenage years and young adult life have been guided by the following "dad-isms," used time and time again. Each of these phrases has helped me to become the independent young woman I am today.

- "Nothing good happens after midnight." Upon receiving my driver's license, my dad advised that I should make my way home around midnight. I never had a set curfew because I trusted my parents' suggestions as to my safety. (This advice also carried over into my college and post-college years!)

- "If you're on time, you're five minutes late." Whether it's for work or play, my dad taught me that being punctual is all about respect.

- "A woman can never be over-dressed." First impressions are key. Whether I'm going on a date or attending a professional function, my dad taught me that if you look good you feel good.

These "dad-isms" taught me the importance of three things: listening, loving, and learning. By listening to my dad, I have learned to reach my utmost potential and have grown to love my father unconditionally. We may not realize it when we are younger, but our parents are the best friends we will ever have.

Don't protect them from all consequences. Allow them to take risks and occasionally fail. Don't be overly concerned with the mistakes they make, but instead focus on the positive. Encourage effort (however slight), and only praise genuine achievement.

Don't be a dominating parent ("too hard") and don't be a doormat ("too soft"). Be a parent who is "just right"—both loving and strict.

* * *

Part I of this book (the first five chapters) focused on how to create a strong foundation for learning. We now turn to part II, which focuses on how to give your children a head start for success in school and beyond. The first thing to do is to stress to your children the importance of education. That is the topic of the next chapter.

Part II

GIVE YOUR CHILD A HEAD START AT HOME

Chapter 6

Stress the Importance of Education

Parents should tell their children that school is important, but they must go further than that. They should tell their kids that *lifelong learning* is important, and that learning doesn't stop at the end of the semester or after the final exam. Learning must be more than simply a way to get grades. It must be a lifelong attitude and a way of life.

The benefits of lifelong learning go far beyond achieving good grades. They lay the groundwork for a successful life. And the topics for children to learn about go far beyond what they learn in the classroom. They include character building, morality, values, and life skills such as how to get along with other people.

BERNA ELIBUYUK

A thin layer of smog wafted through the kitchen window into our small New York apartment as my mother was hunched over the stove cooking a meal. My father was at work, as he usually was, covering the long shift that required him to be up before dawn and carry on through the night. It would be the last day we would be living in the Bronx. The city life that I had known since I was born now exists in my mind as a faint memory.

My parents have always been my strength and motivation, inspiring me to do the best that I can in anything that I set my mind to. Seeing my father working those long hours so that we could live a great life is a strong example that I will continue to carry with me for the rest of my life. He always put my mother and me first, no matter what obstacles

---

were presented. Because of the excessive job requirements my father would shoulder daily, I didn't have the privilege of having my father present during most of my childhood that many kids my age at the time had. We were having financial struggles, but my parents, especially my father, made sure to not make it apparent so that we could live comfortably and free from stress and worry.

I remember that day with the smog in the kitchen, as we had packed up and loaded all of our belongings into the moving van and headed off to Virginia. I would spend my fifth birthday in our new apartment in a quiet suburban neighborhood, as my father continued to work long hours at his new job. He was always a hard worker, ever since he had left his family in Turkey to study at a university in Germany. Working two full-time jobs in a country where he was unfamiliar with the culture, let alone unable to communicate because of the language barrier, was a struggle, my father said.

But he made it through college, graduating with an advanced degree in mechanical engineering, completing his coursework on time, and not falling into debt. His hard work, determination, willingness to strive to reach for his dreams, and constantly excelling in anything that was presented to him, are only a few of the many characteristics that I admire about my father. These traits, combined with the financial and emotional support he and my mother always provided, helped me to excel through all the years of my education.

My father continues to motivate me to pursue my dreams, no matter what they are. Even at a time when I was selecting an undergraduate degree track that was out of the ordinary, he was supportive. Others questioned if I would find any success after graduating from university because I had chosen a major that was new and upcoming. But he continued to support me in any way that he could through college, and now graduate school.

He always reminds me that, "as long as [I am] happy doing what [I'm] doing, and being the best person [I] can be," I will excel and make great strides. I am forever grateful to my father because of this. Even if I can't express my gratitude to him as much as I would like, he continues to give his support and encouragement in even the smallest ways.

All of those small efforts allowed me to grow into a confident young woman, and I have found myself in a successful position as an individual because of the positive examples my father reflected from the beginning. As a father is proud of his daughter, I am proud to have such a wonderful, encouraging, supportive, and loving male figure in my life for a father. I wouldn't change it for anything.

You should have high expectations for your child's learning, and not just in regard to getting good grades. Make it clear that you expect your child to learn deeply and not just temporarily memorize, and that she should value learning for the sake of understanding, not just to pass tests. It is amazing what children can achieve when their parents (and teachers) have high expectations.

Your expectations have a huge impact on your child's success at school. But having high expectations doesn't mean you have to micromanage his life, being what is sometimes called a "helicopter parent" or a "Tiger mom." The best approach is to set high expectations and then step back, so that your child has the opportunity to figure things out on his own.

LAURA GAMSE

While growing up, I never really learned to watch TV. It just wasn't something that would occur to me to do, probably because I never saw my parents watching it. Our only television was a small, archaic box that I never noticed much until friends at school talked about programs I had never heard of. When they found out that I didn't really watch TV, the question was usually, "What do you *do*?" There was never an easy answer.

When I was in elementary school, my grandmother taught me to make intricate flowers out of beads threaded on wires, and I would spend hours with my mother sitting and crafting miniature bouquets, or clay pots, or Sculpey worlds. In second grade I started writing "novels," which my mother would help me bind into little books. She encouraged me to read 100 books during third grade to win a prize my teacher had set up for those of us competitive enough to strive for it. With my mother, everything was achievable. When I set out to write all the numbers between one and a million on one piece of paper, she urged me on. (When my father came home and mentioned that 1,000 didn't come directly after 100, I was disappointed to hear the news.)

Schoolwork was always as important as, if not more important than, any other work in the house. My mother would take time out from writing an article for the *Washington Post* to proofread my papers. If my brother or I needed supplies for a science project at midnight, my father would drop whatever he was doing (which never seemed to be sleeping) to scour the town for a twenty-four-hour supply store.

I remember coming home distressed one Friday, because a project was due the following Monday and I had a seemingly insurmountable load of work ahead of me. My father quickly counted the number of hours available and suggested I get to work. I didn't leave the house that weekend, and worked harder than I ever had before. My mother taught us to aim high, and my father taught us to hunker down and get the work done necessary to accomplish what we had set out to achieve.

Admittedly, the result was two very busy kids, but Mom would tend to drop by during our late nights to remind us that whatever we were up to couldn't be *that* important. Sleeping, eating, or making time for the family could fall by the wayside in our passion for whatever project lay ahead of us, but she kept us grounded.

While parents can tell their kids that lifelong learning is important, no child is going to succeed in school or in life unless she has the grit, determination, and fortitude to work hard, be diligent, and not give up when beset with setbacks and frustrations.

Stanford professor Carol Dweck created the notion of "mindset" and wrote the book *Mindset: The New Psychology of Success.*[1] She draws an important distinction between a "fixed" mindset and a "growth" mindset.

- A "fixed" mindset, explains Dweck, assumes that such basic qualities as intelligence and talent are fixed attributes and can't be changed. Students with a fixed mindset tend to stop trying if they don't do well at something because they believe nothing will fundamentally change. They avoid challenges, fearing that they won't look smart.

- In contrast, says Dweck, a "growth" mindset assumes that basic qualities such as intelligence and talent are malleable and can be improved and developed through hard work, smart strategies, and coaching. Students with a growth mindset are more willing to take risks and wrestle with challenging tasks in a persistent and tenacious way. Such students are not discouraged by mistakes they make, but look on them as learning opportunities. They are inspired, not intimidated, by smart people and try to emulate them. They know that the more they challenge themselves, the smarter they will become. They value learning more than looking smart. They know that they can strengthen their intelligence by working hard.

Dweck's research shows that it is possible to encourage kids to have a growth mindset if parents and teachers act in the following ways toward them:

- Don't praise ability, talent, or intelligence. Doing so promotes a fixed mindset and gives children the message that they have a quality that is fixed instead of one that can grow through diligent effort. It is far better to praise the effort a child makes, and her strategies or choices. Praising the process and the diligence she used will motivate her to persevere.

- Respond in a positive way to failure. Explain to the child that failure is how a person learns and gets better at something. When a child takes on exciting and daunting challenges, it is only to be expected that he won't succeed every time. Making mistakes is actually an opportunity to grow. Setbacks are an integral part of the learning process. They are to be not feared, but welcomed. The brain is growing new connections and getting smarter. Failure is a tool for improvement.

- As a child grapples with difficulties at school, do more than just coax her to keep trying. Help her break a challenge down to smaller components and think through the best strategies and resources for moving forward.

The brain is like a muscle: The more it is used, the stronger it gets. As Salman Khan of Khan Academy says, "The brain grows by getting questions wrong, not right."[2] By learning new things, embracing challenges and being tenacious, a person exercises her brain and makes it more powerful.

BILL GENTILE

My mother left Italy and came to this country with her family in the 1930s so that her father could work in the steel mills just outside of Pittsburgh, Pennsylvania. Though my mother loved school and her studies, my grandfather prohibited her and her four brothers from continuing their education. The men worked in the mills and the women worked at home. Period. So my mother married and produced four sons of her own. It wasn't until later in her life, after my own father passed, that my mother was able to return to school, graduate from college, and become a teacher. She understood something that perhaps my grandfather did not—and that is the value of education. So my mother taught me by example. By hard work. By sacrifice. By persistence and by resilience. And it was very much because of her that I was the first of her four sons to graduate from university. And now I am a teacher, like her.

When a child does well on a test, parents and teachers should say, "You must have worked really hard," rather than, "You must be really smart." Praise effort, not intelligence. The ability to learn challenging material comes from the belief that you can.

Angela Duckworth, a professor of psychology at the University of Pennsylvania, presents insights that resonate with Carol Dweck's research findings. In her book *Grit: The Power of Passion and Perseverance*, Duckworth shows that grit can be fostered and encouraged in children.[3] She argues that success has more to do with grit—passion, perseverance, drive, endurance, and fortitude—than with intelligence.

To raise gritty kids, Duckworth encourages parents to pursue what she calls the "Hard Thing Rule." Everyone in the family chooses one difficult thing to practice, such as yoga, Spanish, long distance running, or playing the violin. Kids with grit are willing to practice and are determined to work hard. They believe in themselves, have a sense of purpose, and are not deterred by obstacles.

Stressing the importance of education and learning is a never-ending task for parents (and teachers). Encouraging kids to have grit and determination by fostering a growth mindset and a positive attitude about failing will help them do better in school and in adulthood.

The key is to praise the effort a child makes, not his innate talent. Children will overcome challenges if they believe that they can and if they have passion, persistence, and purpose.

In addition, parents should make learning a four-season undertaking. Just because there's no school during the summer should not mean that learning ceases. Parents should establish a program of continuing learning in their families. The summer is a wonderful time to go to the library, learn new skills, and implement Duckworth's Hard Thing Rule.

Communicating effectively with your kids about the importance of learning depends on being able to talk to them and listen to them. The next chapter focuses on how to do that.

Chapter 7

Talk with Your Children and Listen Intently to What They Say

If you are like most parents, you are incredibly busy. You have a lot to do, to worry about, and to plan for. This makes staying in close emotional contact with your children challenging. How can you get your kids to talk if you are frenzied and distracted all the time? When you are like that, you probably are giving your children the impression that you are too busy to listen.

Listening sounds easy, but it isn't. It takes effort and time. It is hard to listen patiently to a child when you're preoccupied with scores of other things that are crying out for your immediate attention.

Expect backlash when you don't listen. Children who don't feel listened to or understood by their parents become unhappy. They can potentially display behavioral problems in order to gain the attention otherwise denied to them. Even if they don't act out, kids who do not feel listened to feel unimportant, marginalized, or ignored. This can engender a lack of confidence, feelings of inadequacy, and anxiety.

SEAN GILFILLAN

When I was younger, my father had a demanding work schedule so I would only be able to see him late in the evening when he got home from work, or a few random times during the week. This meant that I was around my mother much more. I would run errands with her, help her around the house, and do various other things with her throughout the day. She was always there for whatever I needed. If I had a school project I needed to work on, I could count on my mom to take me to the store, get all the supplies I'd need, and guide me through the project

---

49

when I needed help. Although she didn't work as much as my dad, she focused her time and effort on making sure my sibling and I always had her to rely on. My dad was also always there for us when he could be. I always appreciated how the two were able to have such demanding lives yet put their work behind them in order to really connect with us and make sure we had a great childhood.

Making kids feel that they are heard and listened to—and therefore valued, loved, and understood—is important. Deborah Fox and Nadine Epstein suggest in a *Washington Post* article that, "It's high time to establish a new 'time' to add to the old staples of 'family time,' 'bed time,' 'dinner time,' and 'floor time': *listening time*."[1]

They write, "Listening time should be a safe time for children to talk. It is not the same as engaging children in conversation, or asking them to listen to adult conversation. It is a time for us to really listen to them."

Of course, kids don't talk just because we want them to. Parents must establish an encouraging and safe climate for conversation. You need to work out the time in the day when your child is most comfortable talking. Maybe it's during the morning walk to school, or at bedtime after reading a book together.

Parents should listen to their child's ideas first. When she is talking, give her focused, exclusive, and undivided attention. Use a warm tone of voice and be prepared to listen for a long time. Encourage her by saying things like, "That's interesting; tell me more," or, "How do you feel about that?"

VANINA HAREL

My father has always been both a source of great support to me and an inspiration. Hardworking and ambitious, I have always seen in him an example. At school, he would be the only one allowed to help me with my mathematics and physics homework. Only he could, because he was the best. He would sit down with me on weekends and explain things with extreme patience, always reassuring in his advice.

When I was studying for my baccalaureate, he helped me create a detailed schedule of work and breaks, with exercise built in between long sessions. I owe to him some of my meticulous organizational skills, assessing how much time each activity will or should take and how to prioritize in order to succeed.

Finally, he has always pushed me to strive to be the best I can. He taught me that, with passion and hard work, anything is possible. His positive reinforcement and support allowed me to become the proactive person I am today, not afraid of taking initiatives.

Listening does not mean giving advice or offering judgments. Once a child seems to have said all she wants to say, be gentle, compassionate, empathic, and thoughtful when responding. Simply listening and trying to understand what is being said, and making it clear that your child's opinions and feelings are important, is a huge gift in and of itself. Often it is all that is needed to help a child solve her problem on her own.

Teenagers sometimes stop talking to their parents because they fear having their ideas dismissed or not taken seriously. One way to overcome this problem is to listen intently without making any judgment and without doing what parents of teenagers sometimes do—probe, nag, pry, blame, advise, or preach.

Communicating effectively with your child is essential if you want to be a happy, successful parent. Your child will talk to you only if he believes you will listen and pay attention respectfully. Parents must listen not only to the words but also to the emotions and feelings behind the words and to their child's body language. Irritability, exhaustion, tears, and shouting are all signals indicating something deeper.

Being an effective listener requires eye contact, concentration, and body language that indicate you are listening. It also requires you to acknowledge your child's right to his feelings by demonstrating that you understand and accept them. When you do this, you show that you respect and value your child's feelings.

A key way to be a good listener is to be an active listener. Active listening is responding to the child in your own words to show that you fully understand what she is saying. For example, "You're feeling angry about the way Brian ignored you," or, "You're disappointed and dismayed you were not selected for the hockey team, but Sarah was." This helps to clarify your child's feelings, as well as shows that you are making every possible effort to understand how she feels.

Effective listening means validating your child's feelings by saying such things as, "It's understandable that you would be upset about being the only one not invited to the party," or, "It makes sense that you don't like that class because the teacher gets angry and shouts a lot," or, "If I were in your position, I would feel frustrated too." Validating what you hear tells your child that his views matter.

ELIZABETH HERZFELDT-KAMPRATH

My father was a huge presence throughout my school career, celebrating my successes and gently challenging me and supporting me through my failures. One impression that stands out to me as the greatest support was how my father saw me as a student. He never failed to see me as an excellent student, smart, hardworking, and successful. I never truly understood this until my high school graduation; my father was beaming with pride at his daughter, valedictorian. He was almost in tears when he embraced me in a hug after my graduation ceremony, congratulating me on my speech that he coached me through. It was often difficult to see or understand, but the success that he saw in me was more valuable than any other support I had in my high school education.

When you are disappointed or irritated with your child, it is helpful to use "I-messages" rather than "you-messages." A you-message criticizes the child and blames him for being at fault. For example, "You are behaving irresponsibly and immaturely by getting home three hours after your curfew without calling me."

An I-message, in contrast, describes how the child's behavior makes the parent feel. For example, "When you get home three hours late without calling me, I get sick with worry that you are hurt or in trouble. I can't sleep because I'm anxious." This message expresses the parent's specific feelings. It does not criticize, assign blame, or find fault.

This chapter would not be complete without a special mention of the challenges faced by girls in our society and the way listening to our daughters can help them. It is extremely important to listen to them because, as author Joe Kelly puts it in *Dads and Daughters*, "a girl's voice may be the most valuable and most threatened resource she has. . . . When she speaks boldly and clearly . . . then she is much safer and surer."[2]

In her book *Reviving Ophelia: Saving the Selves of Adolescent Girls*, Dr. Mary Pipher spells out in excruciating detail how our culture eviscerates girls' voices during adolescence. She writes:

Something dramatic happens to girls in early adolescence. Just as planes and ships disappear mysteriously into the Bermuda Triangle, so do the selves of girls go down in droves. . . . In early adolescence, studies show that girls' IQ scores drop and their math and science scores plummet. They lose their resiliency and optimism and become less curious and inclined to take risks. They lose their assertive, energetic, and "tomboyish" personalities and become more deferential, self-critical, and depressed. They report great unhappiness with their own bodies.[3]

A few pages later, she states the problem even more starkly:

Parents know only too well that something is happening to their daughters. Calm, considerate daughters grow moody, demanding, and distant. Girls who loved to talk are sullen and secretive. Girls who liked to hug now bristle when touched. Mothers complain that they can do nothing right in the eyes of their daughters. Involved fathers bemoan their sudden banishment from their daughters' lives. But few parents realize how universal their experiences are. Their daughters are entering a new land, a dangerous place that parents can scarcely comprehend. Just when they most need a home base, they cut themselves loose without radio communication.[4]

The spunky, self-confident ten-year-old girl turns into a passive, quiet, and timid thirteen-year-old. She silences herself, says author Nancy Gruver, "because she encounters a culture that encourages her to put her own needs second . . . [that] rewards her more for her looks, passivity, and being soft-spoken than for her passions, insights, and beliefs."[5]

Parents, perhaps especially fathers, are in a powerful position to combat these malignant and noxious cultural messages by encouraging daughters not to be silenced. The best way to do this is to listen actively to our daughters and show them that we value what they have to say.

Listening to children with full attention is a foundational parenting skill. Kids need to know that their parents want to hear them fully. Talking with them in a relationship of trust and connection is a goal all parents should strive to achieve. Parents should treat their kids with the same sensitivity, courtesy, and respect that they would show to their best friends.

* * *

Listening to children is important, and reading to them gives parents the opportunity to share thoughts and ideas. It provides rich material to discuss with them. The next chapter focuses on reading to your children.

Chapter 8

Read with Your Child

A passion for reading is one of the greatest educational gifts a parent can give to a child, because it has the potential to transform the child's life. Studies show that kids who learn to read well when young are more likely to succeed in school. This can lay the groundwork for continued success.

Parents should read aloud to their kids every day, ideally for as much as thirty minutes. They should turn off the TV, at least until reading—as well as homework, chores, and family dinner—is completed.

ELIZABETH HERZFELDT-KAMPRATH

My father and I are alike in many ways. We are both stubborn and strong headed, we like to win, and we both are competitive. We both actively try to be the best we can be. This is why it was difficult for my father to watch one of the most challenging matches of my life.

My final tennis tournament of high school was a distinguishing moment for my father (who was my coach) and me. My season so far had been undefeated; my father was incredibly proud of me. The tournament was going great until I was in the round that would qualify me for the state competition if I won. I was confident as I walked onto the court to face my opponent, who had defeated me the year before in this same qualifying game because she was a "getter-backer" (a player who is quick and can basically just get any tennis ball back over the net, which means I made all the mistakes).

The match was going excellently. Everything I'd worked on all season with my father was paying off. I won each round almost without losing any points. Finally I was up 6–0 on the first set and we were switching sides. My dad was so excited with how I was playing, but deep down I was going through the biggest struggle I'd ever faced. I didn't like the place I was in mentally. I was overly competitive and felt as if this match was the only thing that mattered. But I knew there were things that were so much more important. Tennis had consumed my life my senior year, yet I knew it wasn't my passion. I had been accepted to Pacific Lutheran University and had no intention of playing tennis in college, so why did this match matter so much?

My dad didn't know any of this was running through my mind, yet he saw a shift in me. It wasn't until halfway through the next set, when I was losing 0–3, that my dad realized he needed to shift from coach to father. He asked me what was going on and all I could think was that I didn't want to play tennis any more. As a coach this was traumatic for my dad, but as a father he needed to be supportive. So he took a step back and watched me lose the next two sets. I was done with tennis and no longer needed a coach. I needed a father.

Get your child a library card when he reaches the age of seven or so, and make regular—ideally weekly—visits to the library with him to borrow a variety of books and magazines.

Over the summer, reading becomes especially important because it can ensure that all the learning and mental stimulus of the school year doesn't fade away. Encourage your child to read frequently. Find ways to reward him when he does. Kids should read for pleasure and enjoyment, not to please their parents, but setting up some kind of reward system (e.g., earning a quarter for each book read) may still be a good idea to help keep them motivated.

When you visit the library, help your child find fun books. Encourage her to look for books on animals, jokes, stars, sports, science fiction, dinosaurs, biographies, or whatever interests her. And, of course, let her look around the library unhindered, just to explore.

Some children may not immediately be enthusiastic about books and reading. Here are some ways to encourage reluctant young readers to acquire the joys of reading.

- *Tell your child he does not have to finish books he starts.* Children averse to reading can find the idea of reading a whole book daunting. Letting him dip in and out of books at his leisure can make books seem less intimidating. Don't show disappointment when he doesn't finish a book. It could be that the book was too hard to read. Just reading the first page to see if he likes a book is great. The important thing is that he picked it up and looked through it.

- *Help your child discover the fascinating things she can find in books* and the intriguing places to which books can take her—the moon, inside a submarine, swimming with dolphins, car-racing, and so on.

- *If a child can't find anything good to read, show her (or read to her) some of the all-time best-sellers* by such authors as Dr. Seuss, Laura Ingalls Wilder, Judy Blume, Lewis Carroll, Roald Dahl, Shel Silverstein, C. S. Lewis, and J. K. Rowling. Favorite children's books include *Charlotte's Web, Tales of a Fourth Grade Nothing, Island of the Blue Dolphins, Little House on the Prairie, The Outsiders, Shane,* and the *Harry Potter* series. The children's librarian at your local library or school can suggest more well-loved books that your child too may love.

- *Give your child the freedom to read whatever he wants.* Of course you need to make sure it is age-appropriate and not harmful or toxic, but once you have taken care of that, let him read anything, however serious or trifling.

- *Let your child see you reading.* Be a role model. Don't only read after you've put her to bed. You want your child to think of you as a reader. Also make it a habit to talk to her about things you've read and ask her what she thinks.

- *Read aloud to your child.* Let him sit in your lap and see the words on the page. When you read, consciously put on a performance and ham it up. Kids love that! Make it a habit by starting when your child is a toddler, or even a baby.

- *Buy a subscription to a magazine* about a topic that your child enjoys. Again, the children's librarian at your local library will be able to suggest many age-appropriate publications.

ELIZABETH HERZFELDT-KAMPRATH

I knew once I reached ninth grade that my father would encourage me to find a job while I was in high school; I had seen him do the same sort of encouraging with my two older siblings. When it became my turn to find a job, I was frightened and feeling small because I did not know the type of work I wanted to do. I did know that I wanted to balance my schoolwork well with my job. My sister worked at a grocery store and was doing a lot of busy work there, so I knew I did not want a job like that. I thought about fast food and other types of jobs my fellow classmates had and did not think those would fit me either. My father was thinking for me as well, and came up with an idea. His best friend was the executive director at the local radio station, which previously had had high school students work on weekends and evenings as board operators. He quietly inquired with his friend if such positions still existed. Once he found out that they did, he encouraged me to send in my resume. I did so and was asked to come in for an interview. My father drove me to the interview, parked the car, and encouraged me to go in alone, and be calm and clear in my answers. I remember wanting nothing more than for my father to come in with me; I was intimidated and nervous. He made it clear that I needed to do the work on my own, that I needed to have the experience of finding a job on my own and earning the position. I ended up getting the job and was very grateful that my father had pushed me to apply and also to earn the position.

One of the challenges for parents when it comes to reading is how to handle material in children's books that is potentially disturbing or upsetting. For example, material dealing with death, disease, violence, bigotry, animal cruelty, monsters, racism, sexism, and bullying.

It is tempting for you as a parent to do everything you can to shelter your child and hide horrifying content so that she doesn't have nightmares or suffer from irrational and painful fears. Kids do need protection, but they also need to know that the world can be brutal and dangerous. One of the best ways to introduce them to this truth—at the appropriate time, which will vary from child to child—is through good books.

They will see headlines, or pick up stories from older children or siblings, about some outrageous cruelty or horror; so sheltering them forever is both impractical and unwise. At some point, the real world will intrude on their lives. Better for them to be prepared than unprepared. Hatred in its many noxious forms—including violence—is something all children need to know about and deal with.

In an essay in the *Washington Post* entitled, "Why I Let My Children Read Books About Upsetting Things," Suzanne Nelson writes, "So far my children have led sheltered lives, which is exactly why I want them reading books about difficult, uncomfortable topics. They've never experienced violence or prejudice firsthand, but I believe reading about it will broaden their views and open their eyes to others' lives and experiences."[1]

Nelson argues that it is her job as a parent to give her kids love, but "also give them ways to navigate the unexpected and painful."[2]

Children, at the appropriate age, should read books describing alarming and terrifying subjects, such as slavery, the Trail of Tears, the Ku Klux Klan, genocide of Native Americans, and the Holocaust. Reading books—both fiction and nonfiction—by responsible authors about terrible suffering and monstrous evils can help kids grapple with these dark and horrifying topics without being psychologically injured or crippled with fear.

Nelson writes, "By portraying characters facing difficult or tragic circumstances, [books] provide us with tools we need to learn empathy or to survive similar challenges ourselves. Books—especially the ones that keep us up at night; that bring tears to our eyes; that make us angry at injustice, prejudice, and senseless violence—have much to offer, if we're brave enough to accept it. They can guide us on our journey through this imperfect world."[3]

ASHLEY HOLMES

Throughout my childhood and even now, I have always been closer to my mom than to my dad. My mom is a school teacher, so she operated on the same schedule I did until I left for college. This isn't to say my father hasn't helped me, but what he's given me has been by example. My father is quite easily the hardest working man I know. He showed me how to be dedicated to work and yet love your family. He'd work late hours and build up enough time off to give us terrific vacation time together up in the Adirondacks or out west with family. He taught me that hard work pays off.

Even more impressive than his hard work is his passion. My father showed me how to truly care about things by the way he treated my family (especially the dogs), honored his work, and loved the outdoors. He always found a way to balance the three. Starting when I was in high school, my dad really began encouraging my own passions. He not only supported me in everything I did, but added fuel to my fire. When asked what my two sisters and I love most about our father, our answer will be the same. My dad reads a lot of magazines and newspapers, and whenever he comes across an article about something we care about (in my case, animals) he tears it out, writes our name on it, and sets it aside. Coming home to a pile of articles with my name on it always brightens my day. It's such an encouraging thing to be passionate about something and know that your father is now passionate about it too.

Another guide for kids on their journey through "this imperfect world" is to learn stories about their parents, grandparents, and other forebears. In his book *The Secrets of Happy Families*, Bruce Feiler says, "Research shows that kids who know more about the successes and failures of their kin are more resilient and better able to moderate the effects of stress."[4] So look through old family photo albums and tell your kids stories about your childhood, your parents, and your grandparents, including their challenges and achievements.

*   *   *

Reading is vital, but so are other types of learning at home. The next chapter focuses on games and simple science experiments you can do with your children to both fascinate them and give them a head start at school.

Chapter 9

Do Science Experiments and Get Outside

As discussed in the preceding chapter, reading books is an excellent way for kids to explore and learn about science, whether the subject is stars, plants, water, weather, animals, or physics. Another great way to encourage curiosity is to conduct simple scientific experiments at home. These hands-on experiences are especially good for encouraging children to take an interest in science, technology, engineering, and math, the important subjects known as STEM.

Children brim with questions about all kinds of things related to STEM. One way to build on the commendable curiosity of kids and lay the foundation for lifelong learning is to do simple science projects at home using everyday materials. Here are some examples of projects that are easy to do:

- *Clinging balloons*: Blow up some balloons and rub them for a short time on a wool sweater. If you then place the balloons against a wall or ceiling, they will stay there for hours. This illustrates static electricity.

- *Iceberg*: Place a cube of ice in a glass and fill the glass to the brim with water. The ice cube will float and project partly above the surface. Will the water overflow when the ice cube melts? The answer is no. This illustrates that water increases its volume when it freezes and explains why water pipes crack in freezing weather.

- *Identifying hard-boiled eggs*: This is a very simple method for distinguishing a cooked egg from a raw one without breaking the shell. Spin two eggs (one raw, one hard boiled) on a plate. The hard-boiled egg will spin rapidly and continue spinning. The uncooked egg will spin more slowly and the spinning will decrease quickly. The behavior of the uncooked egg illustrates friction, because the loose, liquid content exerts friction against the eggshell.

- *The stable pencil*: Hold a strip of paper over a smooth table edge and place an upright pencil on it. Can the paper be removed without touching the pencil or knocking it over? The experiment works if you pull the paper away in an instant (rather than slowly). This illustrates the notion of inertia or resistance to change.

- *Sugar fire*: Place a sugar cube on a tin lid and try to set it on fire. It's impossible. However, if you dab a corner of the cube with a trace of ash from a burned piece of paper and hold a burning match to that corner, the sugar will burn with a blue flame until it is completely gone. This illustrates how a catalyst works. A catalyst is a substance that speeds up a chemical reaction.

It's easy to create many other home science experiments for kids. One of the best books on the topic is *The Little Giant Book of Science Experiments* by H. J. Press, from which the above examples were taken.[1]

ELAINA KIMES

My dad entered college with the idea of studying law, and left with a Masters of Fine Arts degree. If that does not show you what kind of person he is, I am not sure what will. He showed me that you can find yourself only when you let go of who you think you should be and embrace who you are.

The greatest lesson I ever learned from my father was that genuine understanding means taking a chance on yourself. It is OK to be scared, nervous, or confused after you have jumped into something new. You need to recognize that the authentic creative discoveries, the good parts of life, only happen on the edge of our understanding, not in the middle of it.

Science is an ideal subject to complement a child's natural curiosity. It shows kids how the world works and nourishes the notion that they can tackle and solve problems. It also encourages them to ask challenging and intriguing questions, such as, "Why is there no water on the moon?" or "Where do the stars come from?" or "Why do plants grow?" or "Why do earthquakes happen?" or "Why is the sky blue?" or "How did dinosaurs brush their teeth?" or "How did the pictures get into the TV?" One way for parents to respond to such questions is to help their child find the answers in books or online.

For children, the benefits of learning about science through experiments are significant. They acquire the life skills of solving problems, conducting research, and exercising patience and perseverance. Exploring science can help children form their own opinions rather than unthinkingly accepting the views of others. It can also teach them to think things through—considering what might happen before an experiment begins, creating a hypothesis, and then testing it.

Science should be important to children and their parents for many reasons. There will be many exciting and valuable careers available for children who study science, including those in the fields of medicine, renewable energy, and civil engineering. Jobs in the STEM sector will likely have strong growth and satisfactory compensation.

MEGAN KING

My dad was the kind of student we all envied in school. He was the kid who could have slacked off all semester and then aced the test without ever having opened his book. Don't get me wrong; he is an incredibly hard worker. He bartended his way through medical school, while parenting two small children and enduring a hefty commute between school, work, and home.

I, on the other hand, am the student who has to work hard for what she wants, especially when it comes to standardized test taking. I could study until my brain was going to explode, which was my study strategy for the SATs, but something about the tests' daunting nature and their formality meant that they were not the platform for me to show my strengths. My dad would tell me, "Megan, just think about it like it's a game. It will be fun." And I would always roll my eyes and respond with a, "Sure. Like a game. What is wrong with you??"

Although it pains me to say it, upon reflection I see that he was right. Whether or not I viewed standardized tests as a game, they were. To a certain extent, they were completely trivial. My dad took a unique approach to give me perspective on this, and I am grateful. Standardized tests do not reflect your merit as a creative individual. Your passions, the way you see the world, and finding happiness are far more important. These are all qualities that he has emphasized as holding much more importance than any test result.

While not every child will grow up to be a scientist, engineer, software developer, doctor, or mathematician, even non-STEM specialists such as writers, artists, storytellers, entrepreneurs, and lawyers will benefit from having some STEM proficiency because technology is so pervasive in our society and affects every profession.

Another thing that parents can do to help their kids get more comfortable with science is to take them outdoors. According to Richard Louv, author of *Last Child in the Woods*, today's wired children are suffering from "nature-deficit disorder."[2] His research shows that direct exposure to nature is essential for the mental and emotional health of children, including the ability to concentrate and think clearly.

In his book *Simplicity Parenting*, Kim John Payne writes, "Nature is the perfect antidote to the sometimes poisonous pressures of modern life."[3]

When you take your child outside, especially if you talk about the experience, it opens his mind. He can, for example:

• Taste a fresh tomato or pea from the garden and learn about how plants grow

• Feel drops of rain and learn about the clouds

• Hear birds singing and learn about bird migration

• Feel the wind and learn about the weather and air movement

• Observe an insect and learn about predators and prey

For busy parents, finding time for outdoor activities and nature excursions is challenging. But the rewards are tremendous. If you encourage your child to love nature, she will be more likely to grow up with a strong drive to protect it from abuse. Similarly, having a pet, learning about it, and caring for it can help kids grow up to be more compassionate, caring adults.

Though STEM includes charismatic and renowned tech leaders who are women, such as Sheryl Sandberg and Marissa Meyer, leaders in most STEM fields are men. It is a national tragedy that girls are not involved in science and engineering nearly as much as they should be.

Chelsea Clinton hosts events around the country aimed at getting girls excited about closing the STEM gender gap and making STEM careers appealing for girls. "We're going to have more than a million jobs created in STEM fields over the next decade," Clinton said in a 2014 interview in *Teen Vogue*, "and the only way we're going to fill those jobs with the best and brightest is to not leave a gender behind."[4]

To have women take their rightful and equal place in the professional world, they need to get involved in STEM education when they are young children. Thus parents of girls have a big responsibility.

In addition to books and home experiments, you can encourage your daughter's interest in science by giving her toys that foster creativity, discovery, and learning. Good examples are telescopes, microscopes, magnets, Lego sets, and chemistry kits. MindWare.com has other great ideas for science and technology toys.

KARL KLONTZ

One of the challenges I faced in school was making friends. This is because, having grown up in a family with a diplomat father, I moved to a different country every few years. In one country, I attended three schools in three years—two elementary and a junior high. It was my mother who, in her quiet way, taught me ways to make friends.

I'd just started elementary school in Kathmandu, Nepal, when I gleaned my first lesson from her. It was the early 1960s, a time of turmoil in neighboring Tibet. Thousands of Tibetans trekked over the Himalayan Mountains to seek refuge in Nepal. My mother, active in the refugee movement, invited Tibetans to visit us regularly in our home. It was the Buddhist monks' visits that touched me the most. They came bearing religious artifacts and artwork that they had smuggled from Tibet to prevent authorities from destroying them.

In time, word spread of my mother's interest in Tibetan art. Because the monks sought both a subsistence income and a sanctuary for their art, they streamed to our home. During these visits, our living room became a gallery of sorts, with Tibetan *Thangkas*, prayer wheels, and jewelry displayed across the floor. But it wasn't the artwork that intrigued me so much as how my mother gained the monks' confidence and trust. After inviting them into our house, she made herself present before them and listened caringly to what they said. At first, because she spoke little Tibetan and they knew no English, she relied on sign language, smiles, and body movements to communicate. I often sat on a sofa nearby, watching her interact with them.

While I didn't realize it at the time, I began to incorporate my mother's ways to make friends in each new country I moved to. I learned the importance of reaching out to others even though I was the new guy in town, of being present before others, and of listening intently. Eye contact, body language, facial expressions, tone of voice all became instruments to build friendships. And for that I thank my mother. Friendships, I learned from her, are not inherited and do not come free. Instead, they take work to form, and call for each of us to risk being rejected.

But when friendships seed and grow, they enrich us forever.

You can also help your daughters (and sons, of course) to develop their interest in STEM issues by doing the following:

- Visiting museums, science centers, planetariums, nature centers, and other STEM places;

- Encouraging your children to attend a science camp; for daughters, look to camps focused on STEM activities for girls;

- Encouraging their participation in their school science fair. Teach them the scientific method and then help them succeed with the project, without taking over and doing it for them;

- Involving your children in resolving mechanical or maintenance problems in the house, such as unclogging a garbage disposal, fixing a broken toilet, mending a leaking faucet, changing a door knob, oiling a squeaky hinge, repairing a malfunctioning dishwasher, or painting a stained wall.

*   *   *

Doing simple science experiments and enjoying the outdoors are great boosters for kids. These activities also teach them some life lessons, such as the importance of curiosity and asking questions. The next chapter looks more broadly at life lessons and what parents can do to convey some basic wisdom to their children about how the world works.

Chapter 10

Teach Life Skills

If you want your children to become capable, self-sufficient, and fulfilled adults, you need to equip them with certain life skills that may not be taught in school. Getting good grades alone does not guarantee success in life.

Some of these life skills are foundational (e.g., having good values, emotional intelligence, and a sense of morality). Others are more practical, such as being able to live within your budget and not overspend.

Foundational life skills include:

- *Espousing good values*: When you teach and model such fundamental values as honesty, modesty, courage, diligence, gratitude, and service, it increases the probability that your child will grow up to be a happy and successful adult. You want your child to have a life of joy and accomplishment rather than one of passivity, narcissism, entitlement, indolence, selfishness, and self-indulgence. Look for instances, however limited, when your child exhibits good values and praise her with specificity.

- *Self-discipline and self-control*: If a child has self-discipline, he can keep commitments and promises without a parent having to nag or pester him. Watch for moments when he demonstrates self-discipline, self-control, or impulse control and praise him. For example, if you see him not giving up on a tough algebra problem, praise him for his tenacity.

- *Social skills*: Social skills do not come naturally to most kids. Using good manners, being kind, and not gossiping are all social skills that you need to teach your child. You can role-play on how to thank someone for a gift, how to show appreciation for a compliment, how to meet a new person, or how to deal with hurt feelings. Good social skills also include understanding how to be a friend to someone, how to resist peer pressure, and how to confront a bully. Another important social skill is being self-aware, and using self-awareness to improve behavior and shape social identity, or how a person comes across to others. As always, you should go out of your way to catch your child using effective social skills and praise her with as much specificity as possible. In addition to reinforcing social skills, your praise will help her to recognize those skills in action and understand how to apply them.

- *Teamwork and collaboration*: Teamwork is essential for success in life. For a child who is not part of an athletic team or nonathletic team (e.g., mathletes or chess club), you must step in and help him realize the importance of working well with others in a spirit of collegiality and collaboration. Your child should know that his professional career will be hampered if he doesn't pull his weight, go the extra mile to help his team meet goals, and treat all team members with respect.

- *Critical thinking*: Encourage your child to think critically, to see both sides of an argument, to be unafraid of authority, to stand up to those in power when necessary, to question popular assumptions, and to be skeptical of easy and accepted answers.

You also need to teach practical life skills to your child. Among these are:

- *Eating nutritiously*: Teach your child how to prepare some simple, healthy meals and snacks, so that he doesn't fall back on fast food and take-out.

- *Running a household*: Teach your child basic household chores, such as how to clean floors, dust, vacuum, do the laundry, change a light bulb, and make a bed. It is also important to teach her simple car maintenance, such as how to check the oil level and tire wear. Avoid sexism in assigning tasks and chores.

- *Managing time well and being organized*: Show your child how to keep a calendar and how to note commitments such as dentist appointments, hockey practices, and school tests. A calendar can also be used to track assignments and remind your child when to start preparation for a test, an interview, or a meeting. He needs to learn how to be organized and how to find key documents quickly when he needs them.

- *Budgeting and money*: From a young age, kids are bombarded with messages from the media to convince them to buy, spend, consume, and acquire. Very rarely do they receive messages about the importance of saving or limiting their spending. You have an important role to play here. Teach your child that *wanting* something is not the same as *needing* something. Without that education, teens may leave home for college with a barely controlled and dangerous impulse to consume. Help your child become financially literate so that she knows how credit cards and interest rates work, how to balance a checkbook, avoid large credit card debt, be frugal, and save for the future.

- *Handling emergencies*: Teach your child what to do if she is in a car accident, if she is pulled over by the police, if she ends up going to the emergency room, or if a friend or roommate passes out and your child needs to dial 911. At a young age, your child should memorize her home address and phone number.

- *Giving a presentation*: Everyone at some point needs to get up in front of a group and make a presentation. The more you can prepare your child to speak capably and confidently in public, the better off he will be. For example, while in the car, ask your child to describe as much of what he is seeing as possible within one minute.

- *Running a meeting*: Everyone also will need to run a meeting at some point. You can give your children practice doing this capably by having them take turns running the weekly family meeting (see chapter 3).

ALEX KORBA

My dad was always my biggest fan when I was growing up. I realize that now, at age 22, although my middle school self felt otherwise. A veteran of Vietnam, my dad lectured me on keeping my bed sheets tight enough to bounce a quarter off and getting to bed by 9 on the dot each night. He never allowed me to have a television or a computer in my bedroom, though my shelves had no shortage of books. At the time, I saw all of this as an outrage, but even as I write this I see that all these little annoyances shaped me into the disciplined, well-rounded woman I am today.

Both of my parents had tumultuous childhoods. I believe they saw raising me as their chance to make up for whatever regrets and difficulties they faced in their own pasts. I am an only child, but they came from large families and were the eldest siblings. Because of this, I believe, they were conditioned from a young age to be responsible for others. My mother has lived with spinal cord injury since the age of nineteen, and my father has always been there for both of us, making sure we want for nothing and do not miss out on any of life's experiences.

I owe my dad so much of my worldview. He often took me on week-long road trips. I may have grumbled about them at the time, but now I miss them more than anything. He showed me old films that I criticized at the time for their grainy quality. I now realize they form the bulk of my movie knowledge, and shaped my decision to become a film major. He forced me to manage my time, teaching me to be punctual and stay organized, qualities that many professors and employers have valued in me. The unspoken lessons of my childhood have now started to bear fruit as I step out of college and into the real world. I can never thank my original teacher enough.

In the *Wall Street Journal* in July 2005, columnist Sue Shellenbarger listed the skills college freshmen need, but often lack. They include:

- Asking and negotiating for what they need
- Sharing personal and communal living space
- Exercising basic personal-safety skills
- Showing self-reliance in the face of adversity
- Tracking and controlling personal spending
- Keeping healthy study, eating, and sleep habits[1]

Marilyn vos Savant, author of the "Ask Marilyn" column that appears in *Parade* magazine, wrote an article in March 2001 entitled, "What to Teach Your Kids Before They Leave Home."[2] She described about fifty practical skills (organized into twelve skill sets) that every eighteen-year-old should have. Here is a summary of her list:

1. *Domestic skills*: cook, wash, iron, sew, and clean
2. *Physical skills*: throw and catch balls, swim, ride a bike
3. *Handyman skills*: use basic tools and accomplish simple repair work, such as hanging a picture and painting a room (and cleaning up afterward)
4. *Outdoor skills*: hike and camp
5. *Practical skills*: touch type, set up a computer, drive a car, change a flat tire
6. *Organization skills*: create a budget, balance a checkbook, use a calendar for planning, create a filing system so you can quickly find papers and documents
7. *Social interaction skills*: initiate and maintain a short conversation with a stranger, make a speech, tell a joke, dance
8. *Artistic skills*: draw a simple illustration, sing, play a musical instrument
9. *Care-giving skills*: care for an animal, babysit, care for an elderly or sick person

10. *Orientation skills*: use public transportation, read a map, know what to do if you find yourself in a bad neighborhood

11. *Recreation skills*: play in a team sport (instead of just watching), maintain a fitness regimen, play games (e.g., bridge or chess) that you can enjoy with friends for life

12. *Survival skills*: know basic first aid, CPR, how to take care of yourself if you get sick and you're alone, how to defend yourself.

EMMA KOUGUELL

One of the biggest gifts my dad gave me when I was growing up was an appreciation for storytelling and writing. He always encouraged reading and writing, and he made these areas more exciting for a young girl via father-daughter outings. Each year, we would stock up on books at the local library sales and attend the National Book Festival, where we would pop in to author lectures and grab too many free sticky notes and pens. We also made a routine of people- watching at the airport. While we munched on our Auntie Anne's pretzels, we observed people rushing (or strolling) to their flights. We pulled out our amateur Sherlock Holmes skills as we determined each passerby's story, where that person was going and why, and what type of life the person may lead. At the time, these small events seemed like just that—small things. However, these outings with my dad had a large impact on my performance in school and in shaping my interests and appreciations. For that I am forever grateful.

Now that we are well into the digital age, I would add the following three skills:

1. *How to make face-to-face conversation*: Research shows that obsession with screen time weakens children's social skills, and many kids today don't know how to behave with another person face-to-face. Teach your child how to shake hands, look a person in the eye, smile and carry on an amicable conversation;

2. *How to make a phone call*: Kids don't often talk on the phone because they use text messages and social media with their friends. Teach your child how to conduct a professional phone conversation, or even how to talk with grandparents by phone;

3. *How to properly address an envelope and write a letter*: Kids today often don't know how to write a letter or address an envelope because they use

email or other ways to communicate. Teach your child how to write a letter (both typed and handwritten) so that he knows what to do when, for example, applying for a job or thanking someone in a personal way. The ability and willingness to write a simple, heartfelt thank-you note is a skill every child should have.

Practical skills are important, but it is the foundational life skills that really make the difference. As they enter adulthood, children should:

- Not to be afraid to fail
- Be willing to take prudent risks
- Be able to rebound from setbacks and defeats
- Enjoy hard work
- Appreciate the value of delayed gratification
- Be kind
- Show grit
- Find the good in others
- Tell the truth
- Be considerate
- Keep their lives in balance
- Deal effectively with stress
- Eschew materialism, and
- Set and keep boundaries.

Television, movies, social media, and your children's friends are highly unlikely to teach the important life skills you want your kids to learn. As a caring parent, you need to be proactive and take the initiative here.

SHANNON LAWRENCE

My dad always made an effort to make school interesting and fun. His favorite subject is history, so he would share fun facts with me about historical figures and events. As I got older and I learned about politics and American government, we watched the news together and talked about current events. My family shared many intelligent conversations at the dinner table.

My dad helped me in school by always being willing to answer questions I had about homework, or offering a second opinion on projects and papers.

My dad supported me in school by helping me to learn how to manage my time and workload. School is very important, but my dad wanted to make sure that I could organize my time so that I wasn't doing schoolwork all day every day. He taught me how to take breaks when doing my homework; this actually made me a more productive student.

If you fail to teach your children the life skills described in this chapter, there is a danger that they will be overwhelmed in college by the partying, drinking, overspending, and multiple academic pressures. They may be unable to cope with the resulting stress.

Teaching life skills to children has become a lot more challenging to parents since the Internet arrived and children (and adults) have become obsessed with screens. The next chapter takes a close look at how you can control and limit your kids' exposure to screen time.

Chapter 11

Control and Limit Screen Time

Media and technology have become a powerful second family to children, exerting a significant influence over their emotional, social, and mental development. For adolescents, media use is often centered on socializing with peers, says professor Benjamin Stokes, a social scientist at American University. He says, for example, that teens who are intensively using Facebook are often using that screen time for social affirmation, exploration, and skill development.[1]

At the same time, entertainment companies are spending billions of dollars on movies, television shows, video games, and social media to attract children's attention and loyalty, often producing programs that parents deem harmful and don't want their kids to see.

Parents find themselves edged aside by their kids' screen and social media preoccupations (which sometimes look alarmingly like obsessions) to the point where their influence on their children is diminished. Children's peer-driven and technology-driven lives are making parents feel marginalized. Digital devices have become co-parents, supplying kids with often toxic values and role models.

This undermining of parental authority imposes severe stresses on families, because popular culture is incapable of raising children responsibly and is likely to result in unhealthy development. Technology and the digital age are undercutting the family and weakening the nourishing connections with parents that kids need. But parents can't put all the blame on technology. They themselves must take responsibility. Weak and spineless parenting is part of the problem.

ALISON LEITHNER

When I was in my early teens, school became quite a bit harder for me. I thought it was because I wasn't as smart as other people. Fortunately for me, my mother didn't believe this. She realized that there was one very basic area where I struggled that greatly affected the rest of my studies: study skills. Also fortunately for me, she had some tricks to help me improve.

First, she created a dedicated and organized space for me to do my homework. I was given a desk in the living room that had drawers, pens, pencils, and a wide open space in the middle to spread out whatever I was working on. I was instructed to keep my desk tidy and as free of clutter in the middle as possible. My sister, who was notorious for tidying up around the house, was instructed to leave my desk alone and let me be the only one who used or cleaned it. This ensured that whenever I needed to find something, I was sure to know where it was, since I had been the last person to do something with it.

I was also given a weekly calendar. My mother worked with me on Sundays to plan my week ahead. We made sure that I had budgeted homework time for each of my classes, and had written down when assignments were due and when I would start working on them so that I wouldn't wait until the last minute to start. We also made sure that I had free time left to play or read or do nonschool activities. She understood how important a work/life balance is to everyone—including students—but also knew that if I didn't block off my free time in my calendar, I would forget to take it and get overwhelmed.

These study skills served me well through high school and college. In fact, one of my early calls in my first year of university was to my mother to plan out my weekly study and free time schedule. I continue to use my study skills today, even though I have been out of school for a while. I keep a tidy desk area and ask that no one in my family touch my desk without asking me first. When I'm feeling overwhelmed by all my responsibilities, I look first to my calendar and check that I have given myself a healthy amount of work and play time. If I'm still overwhelmed, I do what I did in the first place—call my mother and ask for her help!

In 2015, Common Sense Media, an organization that studies and rates media and technology for kids and families, released a study showing that media use by children is extraordinarily high.[2] Tweens (ages eight–twelve) use an average of *six hours* of entertainment media per day, and teens (ages thirteen–eighteen) use an average of *nine hours* per day. These numbers exclude time spent using media for school or homework.

Those statistics aren't surprising, given that parents are as addicted to their devices as are their kids. Dr. Catherine Steiner-Adair writes in her disturbing book *The Big Disconnect* that kids are upset by their parents' screen obsessions. They feel neglected and sidelined when parents are constantly focused on their digital devices. She writes, "We read so much about kids tuning out and living online, but that's only half the problem. More worrisome to me are the ways in which parents are checking out of family time, disappearing themselves, and offering that behavior as a model for their children."[3]

Steiner-Adair says that kids, even those who are obsessed with their iPhones and laptops, complain that "their parents are virtually missing in action, routinely either engaged in cell phone conversation and texting or basking in the glow of the computer screen with work or online pastimes."[4] She adds, "Parents' chronic distraction can have deep and lasting effects on their children."[5]

Pediatrician Jane Scott writes, "The undivided attention that children need from us is in jeopardy. Most people just don't realize how much time they're spending online; what feels like a few minutes is often a half hour or more. When we are with our children, we need to be with our children—not with them except for the part of us that's reading emails, tweeting, and checking Facebook."[6]

DIANE MACEACHERN

My mother would famously say, "There'll be no dummies in this house!" When I was three, she taught me the alphabet. Then, when she was cooking dinner, she'd sit me down in the kitchen with a little book. She'd ask me to read the book out loud to her while she was cooking. When I didn't know a word, I'd have to spell it, then reread the sentence to make sure I had learned to actually read the word. I became a good reader in no time, and an excellent speller as well. In school, I was always a few grade levels ahead in reading. Eventually I started winning the school spelling bees. I'm sure those kitchen table reading sessions played a major role in my academic success. And of course, to this day, I love to read.

Setting limits and boundaries for your children is not easy, partly because parents themselves constantly use electronic devices, and partly because the widespread use of digital technology is so new. Parents are dealing with a situation that no previous generation faced.

But while the ubiquity of technology is new, setting limits and enforcing them consistently and compassionately is something responsible parents have done for generations. Kim John Payne writes in his book *Simplicity Parenting,* "Our responsibility as gatekeepers is becoming exponentially more difficult even as it's becoming more critical."[7]

Being conscientious gatekeepers is what effective, loving parents do, even if their kids respond with anger, defiance, profanities, or meltdowns. Responsible parents do not allow, for example, their children to attend sleepovers where inappropriate movies, video games, or websites are viewed.

Setting and enforcing such boundaries is easier said than done, though, because your child might become isolated within friend groups or even mocked. No parent wants that.

But good parents are fearless, decisive, firm, and strong. They avoid negotiations. There is nothing wrong with having kids experience disappointment as a result of parents acting in their long-term best interest.

Meghan Leahy writes, "Rational and kind boundaries [allow] parents . . . to provide safety. We want to help our children mature into a place where they can better handle their emotional and physical lives." Leahy adds, "It's important for parents to remember that technology hijacks brains. Period. That makes technology boundaries tough to uphold, but even more important to create and keep."[8]

You need boldly and unhesitatingly to say to your child, "I love you too much to let you watch a movie (or play a video game, or whatever) that is not good for you."

The report from Common Sense Media concludes that excessive use of screens and mobile devices has led to multitasking that children's brains cannot handle. A high percentage of teens admit that they text, use social media, and watch television while doing homework. The report also concludes that constant attention to devices is making it difficult for kids to have face-to-face conversations or learn empathy.[9]

The technology is here to stay, so here are twelve guidelines for managing it as responsible parents.

1. *Talk with your child about what he is watching and playing.* Teach him to be a savvy media consumer by watching his favorite movies and even playing video games with him and entering into a discussion about them, listening respectfully to your child's views. If you see a video, photo, or post that is beautiful and inspiring, share it with your child and talk about it. Gaming as a family, especially engaging in collaborative games where players are required to work together in teams to win, can be enormous fun, while also offering the opportunity for a family to bond.

2. *Monitor what your child is watching and playing, and limit screen time.* The American Academy of Pediatrics (AAP) recommends that parents

monitor their kids' media diet to help them make wise media choices. If your child is spending too much time posting selfies on Instagram or surfing the web or playing video games, your responsibility is to unplug the device and get her back into the real world. AAP recommends (as of October 2016) severely limiting screen time, including television, computers, and video games, for kids five and under. And for kids six and older, AAP recommends setting consistent limits on screen time, setting limits on types of media, and making sure screen use does not interfere with your children getting enough exercise and sleep. Using screens beyond the AAP recommended limits encourages behavior problems, sleep problems, diminished school performance, and overeating (because of all the sugary food ads).[10] In addition, the Internet and cell phones can facilitate illicit, dangerous, and risky behavior.

3. *Have firm ground rules and boundaries.* Boundaries are important and must be enforced consistently, rigorously, and with kindness. For example, no devices at family dinners, for the first hour after school, and for the last hour before bedtime. No texting after 9 p.m. No TV from Monday to Friday. No TV, computer, or video games in a child's bedroom. No TV when homework is being done.

4. *Never turn on the TV to provide background noise.* It's better for parents and children to watch specific and agreed upon shows, and to watch TV together, so that parents can look for teaching moments.

5. *Keep in mind the character and personality of your child.* Sensitive kids can be traumatized by screen violence and graphic sex, and need to be sheltered.

6. *Protect your child.* Kids are at increased risk on social media. Parents have a duty to protect them. You should have full access, with the child's knowledge, to everything your child is doing online. You should spot-check often, especially if there are warning signs, such as sudden lowered grades, increased irritability, or sadness.

7. *Set a good example and obey the family ground rules.* For example, don't text when driving, at family dinners, or when talking with your kids.

8. *Buy high quality media for your family.* Make them age appropriate by using an established and respected rating system (e.g., the one on the Common Sense Media website).[11]

9. *Reach out to experts for help if you need it.* If a child is faltering in school, failing in relationships, or becoming harmed by excessive use of screens and devices, then contact a doctor or the child's school for help.

10. *Help your child understand the detrimental effects of multitasking.* Kids need to learn the importance of focusing on one task at a time. Multitasking undercuts a child's capacity for sustained concentration, deep reflection, and focus.

11. *Alert your child to the fact that everything he posts online is potentially viewable.* Posts are likely to be open for everyone eventually to see, including malevolent peers and future employers, so kids should be careful.

12. *Create family activities with your children.* Children need to know that they are your highest priority and that you'd rather be with them than anywhere else, nourishing family bonds and memories. Family activities are a valuable substitute for excessive screen time. AAP says that kids need to spend time playing outdoors, reading, pursuing hobbies, and using their imaginations in free play.[12] Family time can be centered around these activities.

In addition to the guidelines mentioned earlier, Benjamin Stokes advises parents to:

- Encourage digital making, not just consumption. He says there's a growing "use gap" between young people who passively consume and those who are makers and learn the tools of production. Predictably, this follows socioeconomic lines, with poorer kids disproportionately consuming. Richer parents send their kids to filmmaking camps and Minecraft summer programs where they learn how to create.[13] This is a tough nut for lower income families to crack.

- As tweens become teens, give them more space but continue to ask questions to show that you care. Tell them what *you* are doing online, so you can be a good role model. Studies have shown that boys in particular may benefit from the time and privacy afforded at online spaces to be more deliberate in engaging with their peers.[14]

Kim John Payne argues that the busyness, stress, and clutter of children's lives, exacerbated by the dominating presence of violence and brutality on screens, is leading kids to have what looks like post-traumatic stress disorder. To Payne, too many kids are fragile, defiant, easily upset, ill at ease, disruptive, fearful, disrespectful, unruly, sullen, and uncooperative.[15]

He contends that adult life is flooding unchecked into kids' lives and that the "sanctity of childhood" has been breached. Kids are suffering from an "undisclosed war on childhood," Payne says. He urges parents to erect "filters to prevent a child's world from being deluged with adult information, pressures, and concerns."[16]

Instagram, Snapchat, YouTube, Facebook, Twitter, and texting encourage children to attach more strongly to their peers than to their parents. Exacerbating the situation is the fact that, in many families, both parents work full time. Thus kids are on their own more, and rely on their peers at a much earlier age than in previous generations. Parents need to be more authoritative, assert themselves more strongly in their children's lives, and form stronger attachment and closeness to their kids. Children need a close, loving, and sympathetic connection with their parents, and they need their parents' attention.

Way back in 1996, author Mary Pipher wrote *The Shelter of Each Other*, in which she argued that, because of TV and other digital devices, children were no longer being socialized by their parents, and that technology was destroying families. She persuasively made the case that home life was being displaced by electronics, and that kids were being bombarded to such an extent by TV and the Internet that they were being taught to be "self-centered, impulsive, and addicted." They were losing their social skills, exhibiting bad manners, becoming materialistic, and showing low emotional intelligence.[17]

Unfortunately, because of the unstoppable proliferation of screens, the problems facing families have severely worsened since Pipher wrote her book. Our use of screens is putting our kids at risk. Most children are now learning about sex from Internet pornography. It is as if society no longer wants to protect childhood. If parents, who are invariably stressed and exhausted, don't have the time or willingness to teach their children values, the media in which kids are marinating will do it for them—and the results will not be what parents want.

DAVID MULLINS

I owe much of my organizational skill to my mother. I have a distinct memory from sixth grade, when I had a project due at the end of the month. Because the assignment wasn't due the next day, I didn't think about it. My mom quickly caught on and, as a school administrator and educator herself, got a plan together. There was a skill I needed to practice.

She printed out a calendar—a large one—and placed it on my desk. It was so large that it covered my desk, and I would always see part of that calendar no matter what I was working on. There were certain days with tasks scribbled in, such as, "complete two paragraphs," and other days with nothing. I loved those blank days. I even tried to shuffle some around to cash in all at once—missing the point at the time—and I was caught red-handed.

It was hard for me then to see the big picture, but it's easy now to look back and understand how this project-within-a-project has helped me. I always pride myself on being extremely organized—in school, in my profession, and in life. I owe that to my mom. I've succeeded in these areas because of a skill that is now second nature. Back in college, I would always look ahead. I would see what I had time for—whether that meant an assignment, an outing with friends, or even my favorite TV show. I would schedule it all in.

The ultimate result has been a lack of forgetfulness, a lack of that "I completely forgot" moment that many might recognize. I didn't have those moments. I still don't. And I love that. I can see what I'm working on in a larger context—and I still make to-do lists for myself every week. I don't plan every little detail like I did in school, but the important stuff is on there. For example, writing this entry. It's currently at the top of the list.

Thanking my mom is next.

To obtain an expert viewpoint on the topics in this chapter, I reached out to professor Lindsay Grace, the director of American University's Game Lab and Studio. He read this chapter and then observed:

Your recommendations seem appropriate. I would argue, however, that one of the things missing is an acceptance of digital socialization. In short, keeping your children out of the loop for such socialization shortchanges their potential. Monitored use of the Internet *is* essential, but it's also important to recognize that children become teens and adults. As such, familiarity with these technologies, netiquette, and the social support groups that come from these communities is also an important part of their lives.

In some cases, online activities can provide community where there is none. Consider, for example, teens who struggle with gender identity, or more simply, children with distinct hobbies. I believe that too often people view the online environment as an encyclopedia with a collection of dangerous red-light districts. But it's also a place to develop and sustain communities. It's a place of diverse interests and affinity groups. Lastly, lots of the work of daily life happens on the Internet. Familiarity and comfort with the Internet and online communities is essential. This is apparent in everything from our inability to discern fake news from real news to understanding and mitigating trolling, online bullying, and the myriad of pro-social (and anti-social) activities that exist in digital communities.

The same goes for game communities. Beyond the traditional benefits of games cited (e.g., proactive problem solving, creative practice) there are also communities of players that create hobby communities in everything from the much championed STEAM interests (e.g., coding, modifying existing games to make new ones, and technical work) to the creative communities like costume play and fan fiction writing.[18]

Despite Professor Grace's positive attitude toward screens, I strongly believe that parents need to reduce the quantity of time their kids spend on cell phones, TV, computers, tablets, video games, and so on, so that they can spend more time bonding with parents and siblings, reading books, playing outside, engaging in imaginative play, being creative, and socializing face-to-face with friends.

* * *

So far in this book we have discussed how to create a strong foundation of learning and how to give your child a head start at home. Now we will turn to part III and how to support your child at school.

Part III

SUPPORT YOUR CHILD
AT SCHOOL

Chapter 12

Be Present at Your Child's School

Parents can have a major impact on their child's success at school. You need to be deeply involved in your child's education to ensure that she is getting properly educated and that her school is an effective learning environment. Developing good relationships with your child's teachers is essential. Even though you are busy, you must make time to get to know the teachers; it is crucial.

Teachers know that a harmonious and cooperative relationship with a child's parents will strengthen the connection between home and school, and thus the child's learning. Once a teacher attaches a child to a parent's face, that child becomes more important to the teacher. Teachers know the importance of working with parents as allies.

Reach out to your child's new teacher at the first opportunity. By forming a sound relationship with teachers early in the school year, you will be better able to deal with any problems that arise later in the year.

CHRIS PALMER

When I was about eighteen years old, I came home for leave after joining the Royal Navy. My father greeted me with a perfunctory handshake, and then immediately asked me about my grades. Rather pleased with myself, I told him they were above average—mostly As, with a few A minuses and B pluses. His face darkened. "For God's sake, you can do better than that," he snapped angrily. "You *have* to do better than that. You should be getting nothing but As. Your grades

---

are unacceptable." I was shocked by his fierceness, but from that point on, I resolved never to get anything less than As. His demands pushed me to achieve what I'd previously assumed were impossible goals—and after that conversation, I always did my best and earned virtually perfect grades.

Virtually all schools hold family nights or open houses for parents to visit the school and meet their child's teachers. These events not only give parents and teachers a chance to meet. They also allow parents to network with other parents whose children share the same teachers. This can be helpful later in the school year when you might need to reach out to other parents for advice.

Finding out what your child will be learning, how a typical school day is organized, and how the teacher likes to communicate with parents (written notes, newsletter, phone calls, email, or social media) shows your child that you attach value to her education. Teachers appreciate parents who show an interest in what is going on in school.

Another chance for parents and teachers to meet and strengthen their partnership is at parent-teacher conferences. This is an opportunity for each side to listen to the other and to share ideas on how to help your child learn. Come to parent-teacher conferences prepared with questions, including:

- What does my child enjoy?
- What are her strengths?
- What are her weaknesses?
- Is she learning the material satisfactorily?
- Is he engaged in the material?
- Is he working at grade level?
- What will he be learning over the rest of the school year?
- What are his teacher's expectations for homework?
- Is she getting her homework in on time?
- What is the best way to contact you?
- What can I do to help her learn more?
- How is she doing socially in the class? Does she get along with the other kids?
- Is he participating in class?

Also ask the teacher about any concerns that your child seems to have concerning the class. If anything is bothering her or causing her anxiety and worry, this is the time to bring it up. The teacher will let you know if the topic should be the focus of a separate meeting.

CHRISTINA PALMER

I was a very shy child. I hated "show and tell" days in kindergarten and *never* wanted to participate in them. My dad knew this. He didn't get angry or make me feel bad, but got a big empty plastic box and starting collecting interesting things in it. Each week, the night before show and tell, he would take out the box and we would do a practice a show and tell. While I still didn't particularly enjoy doing show and tell, this helped me feel more prepared, so I could participate with more confidence.

CHRISTINA PALMER

Growing up, I remember Sundays being our day for both "family meetings" and "teacher/student" time. In our family meetings, we would take turns being in charge and would discuss our plans for the week, our biggest upcoming challenges, and any family conflicts. While we didn't always love going to family meetings, they were a vital part of our family ritual and taught us each a lot about leadership, working as a team, and setting goals.

Later in the day, we did "teacher/student." We would have to a pick a topic to "teach" our dad about. It could be anything we had learned the week prior, but we had to make sure we knew it well enough to teach it. This helped me learn.

Don't forget to thank the teacher and to express appreciation for all his hard work and dedication. You may have some stressful issues to discuss with him, so these soothing words, assuming they are said with sincerity, will help ease any tension.

NICK PAPADIS

One of the most memorable moments of my mom having an impact on my education was when she told me I had been accepted to American University (AU). For a bit of background, my family is a very small one. My dad passed away when I was a freshman in high school, and I am an only child. This meant that my leaving to go far away for school would be very tough for my mom.

I had to decide whether to attend Clemson University or the University of South Carolina—both of which are an easy drive from my hometown—or go to AU, which was my top choice, but also very far from home. To make the decision more difficult, I had been offered very good scholarships to both of the in-state schools. But all through high school I had wanted to get away from my hometown and go to a major city for college. I had finally been accepted to a school I really wanted to attend: AU.

I had to choose between staying near my mom at a less expensive school or going to my dream school and taking out large loans. At this point, my mom said something very memorable to me. She told me that, while she knew it would be hard for her if I left and was far from home, she wanted me do the best thing for my education. She told me to leave and go to AU.

The thing that meant so much to me about her saying this was that I could tell how hard it was for her. She encouraged me to choose AU because she believed it was the best decision for my future.

CHRISTINA PALMER

When I was in high school my dad would drive me to school most mornings. As a moody teenager, this was not something I particularly enjoyed. My dad had a long morning commute and his car was piled up with books on tape: self-help books, books about the Civil War, biographies of Benjamin Franklin, and so on. Sometimes he would put these on and we would listen together. He called this his "University on Wheels," which for some reason made me laugh (and those days he had a hard time making me laugh). While I never would have told him this at the time, I found his University on Wheels secretly inspirational. Having him role-modeling constant learning and self-improvement made me want to do the same.

Knowing what is being taught in school allows you to guide the conversation at family dinners to material your child is studying. This could make a significant difference in your child's performance.

In addition to developing strong ties with teachers, parents can be present in the school in many other ways. You might chaperone field trips to zoos and museums, lead nature walks for science classes, referee on field days, read aloud to the class on story day, be an after-school tutor, help out in the school library, volunteer to help in class, or coach an after-school sport.

When your child sees you spending time at school and being interested in what is happening in his class, you show him that education matters.

If you receive a report card from school saying that your child cannot focus in class and implying that his behavior is consistent with attention deficit hyperactivity disorder (ADHD), you should not immediately assume that your child would benefit from medication. Pediatrician Chad Hayes says that you should first ask your child *why* he is distracted in class and what would help him do better.[1]

JENNY PALMER

I have always been able to count on my dad 100 percent to be there when I need him. When I was growing up, no matter how busy he was, he would always make time for me. If I ever asked him for anything, I knew I could count on him to help me right away or let me know when he would be able to help. He spent a ton of time, for example, reviewing draft after draft of my college admission essays and providing feedback. His reliability and trustworthiness made a huge difference to me.

It could be, says Dr. Hayes, that the child doesn't need medication for ADHD so much as less sugar in drinks and desserts, less television, fewer video games, more exercise, more nutritious meals, fewer angry fights between his parents, more challenging work, better glasses, more sleep, or whatever. Or he might be a victim of cyberbullying, physical bullying, or anxiety attacks. Not everyone who struggles in class has ADHD.

If getting easily distracted and losing focus is a real problem, then perhaps a visit to a pediatrician or psychiatrist might be a good idea, and perhaps meds might help. But Dr. Hayes says medication should be a last resort. Of course, talk with your child's doctors and don't be afraid to ask for a second opinion.

JENNY PALMER

My dad used to give me math problems while we were eating breakfast before school. He didn't care when I was "supposed" to learn things. I remember that he taught me how to solve algebra equations when I was in around third grade, putting me light years ahead of the other kids when we finally got to algebra class in seventh grade. These mornings were actually very fun for me! The math problems were games, and my dad was very encouraging.

ELIZABETH RUML

I don't recall any particular hands-on assistance from my parents when I was growing up, but they set a good example by being what today is called "life-long learners." Perhaps more important, though, is that my parents conveyed to me the strong message that getting a good education is valuable almost beyond measure, not only in economic terms but also as preparation for fundamental joy of life. It was always understood that I would attend college and graduate school if I wanted or needed to, and I was able to finish my education without incurring any debt.

In his book *Girls on the Edge*, Dr. Leonard Sax writes, "The scariest thing about all these kids being diagnosed with ADHD is that the medication most often prescribed for ADHD—Adderall, Ritalin, Concerta, Metadate, and Focalin—will work even if these kids don't have ADHD."[2] The response to treatment can be misleading because the positive results of using these meds may lead parents and teachers to believe the child had ADHD when that may not be the case. Medications improve the attention and focus of children *without* ADHD, but prolonged use of these drugs, says Dr. Sax, may make a child apathetic, disengaged, and unmotivated.[3]

How else can you be present in your child's school and his education? Here are some ideas.

- Find out about progress reports and how to access them

- Help your child get his homework done and create a study area for him at home

- Create the expectation that, at the family dinner, your child will tell you one thing she learned in school that day

KIMBERLY PALMER

One night as a junior in high school, I had reached what was then my peak of stress: I had SATs to study for, a massive history exam, a swim meet and a poem to memorize. As I arrived home around 6 p.m., starving and cranky after an exhausting swim team practice, I just wanted to cry. I had no idea how I was going to get everything done.

For some reason, my mom was out that night, so it was just my dad in charge, taking care of my two younger sisters and me. When I told him I was paralyzed with stress, he very calmly told me that everything would be fine: We would simply tackle one thing at a time. Starting with the poetry memorization, we did just that, crossing the tasks off our list as we accomplished them.

I'm not sure how he managed to help me so much when he was also juggling dinner time and caring for two other children but, in my memory, I had his complete attention. My problems were important enough for him to focus on, and that alone helped me to relax and face them. Today, I still take the "one task at a time" approach when my to-do list feels overwhelming.

- Monitor (and limit) your child's television, video games, and Internet use, so that he has time for reading, homework, etc.

- Encourage your child to read by reading to her and having her read to you

- Demonstrate a positive attitude toward education and its importance

- Encourage your child to be responsible and to work independently

- Encourage your child to use the library

- Post your child's school calendar at home

- Review the contents of your child's backpack each evening (if your child is young) and ask questions about what you find there

- Help your child to determine a regular time each night by which his homework will be completed

- Make each weekday morning a calm, peaceful experience by preparing the night before—getting out the clothes to be worn, planning the breakfast and bag lunch, organizing the backpack, etc.

- Be active in your child's extracurricular activities, by attending sports events, band performances, art shows, or whatever the events may be

* * *

It is important for you to be present in your child's school, but sometimes more is required. Parents must become advocates for their kids. That is the topic of the next chapter.

KIMBERLY PALMER

My dad did not give us overly positive feedback when we asked him to help us with writing assignments. In fact, I often dreaded showing him my written work because he would have dozens of suggestions for ways to improve it. At times, I found this quite frustrating, but it also made me commit to improving and not settling for thinking my work was "good enough." That kind of pursuit of excellence stuck with me, too.

Chapter 13

Be an Advocate for Your Child

In addition to being present in your child's school, sometimes it's necessary for you to be an advocate.

For example, you can help ensure that your child receives his fair share of especially good teachers. In every school, there are caring and highly capable teachers who have the ability and creativity to inspire even those children who seem to have no interest in learning.

The school is likely to resist your efforts to favor one teacher over another because it wants to fill every teacher's class. Nevertheless, you owe it to your child to try. Approach school officials well before school begins, and make the case that you want your child to be placed in a specific teacher's class. You won't always get your way, but it's worth the effort because highly effective and caring teachers are hard to find and can transform kids' lives.

Regardless of the specific teacher, once school starts, you need to find out how your child is doing. Ask your child's teacher. If the teacher says she is not keeping up with work, you should discuss with the teacher what steps can be taken to help your child.

It is important to take swift action before your child gets too far behind. Find out as specifically as you can what exactly is happening. Is the problem with the class material, with another student or a group of students, or with a teacher? Share what you find out with school administrators. If you suspect your child might have a learning disability, see your family doctor or the school counselor to get help finding the proper support.

Your child might have a teacher who is mediocre or even incompetent. In that situation, you need to be a strong advocate for your child.

- Take action immediately. If you wait, the semester will be half over and the school may try to persuade you to stick it out.

- Meet with the teacher and be as calm, respectful, and direct as possible about your concerns. Your child may continue to interact with the teacher you are complaining about, so be polite and do your utmost to maintain a good working relationship with him. Hopefully you'll see improvements. If not, put your concerns in writing and take them to the next level. The concerns might be child-related—as in, my child is having trouble grasping the material—or teacher-related—as in, your explanations are confusing to my child.

- Talk to other parents to see what they think. If they agree and you can cite their support, the school will have to pay more attention to your concerns.

- If there is no improvement, tell the school that your child has to be moved to another class before any long-term damage to her education occurs. If the teacher can't keep order in the class, behaves in negative ways, or is ignorant about the material he is meant to be teaching, then that teacher is incompetent and your child is in an unacceptable situation.

- Find out if the school has tutoring programs that might help. Also check with your local library; it may have a homework center where children can get help.

If the teacher is a problem, you must speak up because you may be the only advocate that your child has. This is not being a helicopter parent. This is being a responsible parent.

CHUCK SALTSMAN

My parents were voracious readers. Some of my earliest memories are of my mom reading next to me in bed and my dad pointing to the big dictionary on the bookshelf, telling me to "look it up" when I encountered a word I did not know. My parents came from the generation that believed everything you could learn was available in books and magazines. We had *National Geographic* magazines dating back decades. We had books by Arthur Conan Doyle, Joseph Conrad, Charles Dickens, and many more. I explored the world from my house before I even went to school.

I saw the Monterey Bay Aquarium on the cover of *National Geographic*, read the article about it, and knew I had to work there someday. My parents also bought me all the art and camera equipment they could afford, took me to museums and lectures, and did their best with a kid who knew he wanted something in life that was very specific but couldn't quite get in suburban Detroit.

Learning to read young and developing a love for books and science and exploration: that is what my parents gave me as best as they could, even if they didn't know exactly what they were preparing me for. They did a fine job.

By making learning a priority, you show your child that success at school is important. High expectations from you will make it more likely that your child will come to value and love learning.

Another area where parents may need to be advocates, especially the parents of girls, has to do with sexism in coed schools. Parents can put their daughters into single-sex education or otherwise advocate for fair and supportive treatment in a coed environment.

Dr. Myra Sadker and Dr. David Sadker, former education researchers from American University, observed teachers in classrooms at all grades for more than twenty years. They found that, while teachers support gender equality and believe in it, they unintentionally reinforced gender stereotypes and ran their classes on gender assumptions that fetter and limit girls.[1]

The accumulation of these unintended sexist messages can reduce a girl's self-image and self-identity to the point where her self-confidence is low and she no longer believes she is competent to tackle technology, science, tools, numbers, and so on.

Girls tend to be praised more for the appearance of their work, and for being unobtrusive, meek, and unassuming. Boys are chosen to answer questions more frequently and are more likely to shout out answers without being called on. When girls shout out answers, they often are instructed to raise their hands first.

KIMBERLY PALMER

When I was young, my dad always worked in his study at home after we went to bed. I would hear him dictating into his phone or shuffling papers late into the night. He also brought us to his office and showed us what he was working on. Seeing his passion for his work, combined with his obvious enjoyment of it, helped show us that we could find work one day that we would find satisfying, too.

Years of research consistently shows that classroom teachers, both men and women, pay most attention to boys who misbehave, call on girls less often than boys, and give girls less help. These are things that teachers are blind to and in fact don't believe they are guilty of doing until someone videotapes their class and points it out. Most teachers are eager to change their gender bias once they see it.

When girls get less recognition for their academic abilities, and when they see boys getting more attention in class, it leads to girls' voices being silenced. This is one reason that, on TV programs such as the popular general quiz show *It's Academic*, the teams from coed schools are dominated by boys. It's why many girls don't have the self-confidence to push themselves forward into school leadership positions.

Despite the progress women have made in the last 100 years, our culture is still toxic to the healthy development of girls. Parents and teachers need to encourage girls to find and nurture their real voices, the ones they had in preadolescence, and not always to say what they think others want to hear.

While women have made inroads in male-dominated fields over the last few decades, such as law, business, politics, medicine, and engineering, they are nowhere near achieving equity. Major discrepancies still exist.

Many educational experts feel that girls are better off, especially in high school, in classes or schools that are single-sex rather than coed. Dr. Sax writes in *Girls on the Edge*, "Certainly there is plenty of evidence that girls do better academically in an all-girls classroom."[2]

As Mary Pipher showed so powerfully in her book *Reviving Ophelia*, adolescent girls often seem to lose themselves once boys enter the scene. That is heartbreaking.[3] The importance of girls' achievements, strength, self-confidence, vitality, and health can get overwhelmed by the opinions of boys. Mixing adolescent boys and girls together in a coed school produces social tensions, stresses, and anxieties.

The sexist environment in a coed high school encourages girls to focus on their appearance. This discourages academic achievement and character development, and encourages superficiality and submission to boys' opinions. Hence the appeal of all-girls schools, especially ones where school uniforms are required.

At a coed high school, what tends to matter if you are a girl is who likes whom, who's wearing what, who's "hot," who's "cool," who's pretty, who's cute, and who's fashionable. Girls tend to be passive and quiet. At girls-only schools, they can live out loud, be players, and blossom. In an all-girls class or school, girls are more likely to be verbally expressive, emotionally expressive, enthusiastic, energetic, and lively.

Girls do better in single-sex settings because they are free to take risks that they are unwilling to take in classes where boys are present. Pioneering research by Dr. Carol Gilligan, Dr. Myra Sadker, Dr. David Sadker, Dr. Catherine Steiner-Adair, and many others has shown that girls learn best when they are in a place that develops their confidence, self-esteem, capabilities, life skills, and sense of being connected. That means a place without the agitations brought on by the presence of boys. In single-sex classes at the high school level, girls have greater opportunity to hold leadership positions and develop skills without the intense competition usually found in coed settings.

Without the distraction of boys, girls can be themselves, build on their strengths, and be more likely to find success. They can find out what their best selves can be and learn that nothing need stand in their way. They can take center stage instead of being relegated to the periphery.

They can find their voices, excel in academics, and get the best preparation possible for successful and meaningful lives. They can explore, experiment, and role-play without wasting time thinking about how their male peers might view what they are doing. Time in class is spent learning and growing, not worrying about what boys think.

Girls need to be told and made to believe that they can be heads of organizations, presidents of companies, universities, and countries, and that their career aspirations can be as bold and ambitious as any boy's aspirations. Single-sex education can help achieve this.

My preference for girls to attend all-girls schools, especially for high school, is based on my personal experience with my three daughters and is simply my opinion. Many advocates for the opposing viewpoint—coed schools—make powerful arguments about not sheltering girls from a male-dominated society, and the benefits of all children learning to socialize in coed settings. And, of course, there can be toxic relationships between girls at all-girls schools that are as damaging as toxic relationships between boys and girls at coed schools.

CRYSTAL SOLBERG

When I was growing up, my family ate dinner together every night without fail. It was never questioned. It was just a part of our routine—although I doubt it was ever easy to get seven children and two adults all together!

We used to play a game at dinner. The object was to name at least two things we learned that day. All seven children and two adults were required to answer with facts, not opinions. Not only did this force each of us to reflect on our day. It also encouraged us to engage in the lessons we were taught both in school and out.

We ate together and we learned together.

Moreover, for many girls, there will not be an all-girls option. There are things the parents of these girls can and should do. They include:

- Encouraging teachers and school administrators to create girl-focused leadership opportunities;

- Supporting strong girls-only activities in the schools, such as sports, clubs, and girls-mentoring-younger girls service projects;

- Looking for out-of-school programs that provide leadership opportunities for girls, such as girl scouts and sports teams;

- Advocating for all-girl classes in coed schools wherever possible.

Parents of girls have a particular responsibility to look out for the long-term interests of their daughters, and make sure they are given every opportunity to advance academically and in extracurricular activities.

During school visits, parents can observe how many male and female role models are represented on the walls, bulletin boards, and displays. If there is a disproportionate number of men, point that out to the teacher. During a parent-teacher conference, parents should watch for unintentional red flags from the teacher. If, for example, he extols your daughter's penmanship and good manners in class, then make it clear that you want her to excel academically.

Parents should teach their daughters to call out sexism and gender inequality whenever they observe it, including if they detect it when chores are assigned at home. And of course it is important for parents, especially mothers, to model self-assurance, confidence, and self-assertiveness.

* * *

One area where parents have a significant role to play is in creating circumstances at home that allow and encourage your children to get their homework done. This is the subject of the next chapter.

Chapter 14

Help with Homework

All students have homework, and it is important that they have the self-discipline to focus on getting it done to a high standard by the deadline without indulging in procrastination.

Homework is well-intentioned. For the most part, it is valuable—even invaluable—and students benefit from it. It is your job to help your children succeed at getting it done.

Occasionally homework might be excessive or overly stressful (especially for young kids), but it nonetheless teaches self-discipline, delayed gratification, and the virtues and pleasure of diligence. It also teaches many of the skills needed to succeed in life, including good work habits and the ability to follow directions.

The National Education Association[1] and the National Parent Teacher Association[2] both support the "10-minute" rule: a daily maximum of ten minutes of homework per grade level. Fourth graders, for example, should do about 40 minutes of homework each night.

ANA SOTELO

In November of 2013, I was working on my thesis film in Washington, D.C. Or at least that's what I would tell others—and myself—that I was doing. I had shot the film in June the year before and had spent the next ten months or so attempting to piece together and edit it. Writing narration, organizing scenes and sequences, choosing a look, deciding on a narrative thread—all these tasks had to be done, and the clock was ticking.

When people asked about my progress, I would respond by saying, "It's still in my head" or "I'm uninspired right now." Meanwhile, I would spend days doing activities I thought would help me find "inspiration." I would watch films, read books on films, and go through my school notes. Nada. I would take walks in the woods, hoping that surrounding myself with nature would bring better ideas. Nada. I would meet up with peers and see their progress. I would ride the Metro from one end of the city to the other, observing riders and trying to write narration based on that, but eventually I'd come home, again, with nada.

One afternoon, I returned from one of these outings and found my dad at home, working at the dining room table. I studied him and envied him. He sat absorbed in his work, with that look on his face that I so yearned for—inspiration. He looked up and asked about my progress. I collapsed onto the couch and began complaining about how I had no inspiration, and how without that I could get nothing done. He simply smiled and asked me to get up. He pulled a chair next to him, began writing on a Post-it note, looked at me and said, "This is how you will get things done." I looked at the yellow post, excited to finally discover the secret to inspiration, and read: "Ass in Chair." I turned around, puzzled, and he responded, "I promise, that's it." So for the next weeks, I sat myself down, the Post-it stuck to a corner of my computer, and began completing the necessary tasks. Sure enough, by the end of the year, my thesis was finished and handed in.

Here are nine things you can do to support your child's mastery of homework.

1. MAKE SURE YOUR CHILD HAS AN ORGANIZED PLACE TO WORK

Create a study center at home where your child can comfortably study and do homework effectively. It should be equipped with a desk, a chair and good lighting, and should be free of distractions (e.g., TV). Especially for younger children, the study center should include space for a parent to join the child for questions and discussions.

Stock a homework box with all the supplies your child will need, such as pencils, erasers, paper, a calculator, a stapler, paper clips, and tape. Older children will also need an assignment notebook and planner.

Minimize clutter in the study center, and more generally throughout the home. Messiness and disorganization exacerbate the natural stress and chaos of family life and make learning more difficult. Disorganization is a barrier to success in school, and to being fully engaged in life.

The purpose of de-cluttering isn't to be tidy for its own sake, but rather to enable your child to find the things she needs quickly and efficiently when doing her homework. If your child's study center is de-cluttered, organized, ordered, and functional, she will be more likely to reach her full potential when doing her homework.

2. HAVE A SCHEDULED TIME EVERY DAY TO DO HOMEWORK, AND MAKE IT A PRIORITY

Set aside a homework time—the same time each day—so your child gets into a rhythm of completing his assignments. A predictable routine will get kids in the habit of settling down quickly to do their homework.

If your child starts his homework without being told, praise him very specifically for doing that. Praised behavior is likely to be repeated.

3. ASK QUESTIONS TO SHOW INTEREST IN WHAT YOUR CHILD IS LEARNING, AND MONITOR HER HOMEWORK

You need to show your child that homework is important. Ask her to teach you what she is learning. As author Stephen R. Covey pointed out, teaching a topic is the best way of learning it.[3] Offer to go over her homework, and praise her for the effort she has made.

Initiate conversations with your child about what she is learning in class. Listen to her opinions and views. Get to know her values, her character, and what matters to her. Both you and your child can be stimulated by these conversations. They will help your child think about important issues and articulate her opinions.

If a child is enthusiastic about learning, encourage her to do more than the minimum. High achievers should never be discouraged from doing extra homework.

4. LET THE CHILD EXPERIENCE SOME FRUSTRATION BEFORE YOU STEP IN TO HELP

Don't start helping your child as soon as you see him struggling. Be patient. It is in struggling that he learns. Step back and don't interfere until the child seems close to giving up. By allowing the child to viscerally feel frustration, you are teaching him not to give up when the going gets tough. You are also showing that you are confident he can master the material on his own.

The key is to set high expectations and then interfere as little as possible. To the extent you can, let your child figure out problems on his own and take full responsibility for getting his homework completed and submitted.

Distinguish studying from learning. Just because your child spends a lot of time studying does not mean he has learned the material. Quiz him, if you are able to, to see if he really knows it.

5. NEVER DO THE WORK FOR YOUR CHILD

If it looks like your child may give up, then intervene, but in a gentle, minimally intrusive way. Perhaps check to see if she has read the instructions properly, or pose a question to get her thinking in the right direction.

If your child asks for help, encourage her first to explore other resources, such as a dictionary or encyclopedia. Help her to become independent and solve her own challenges and problems. If you always rush in to help, you will likely raise a child who is overly dependent on you to get homework done, to get organized and focused, and to get things turned in on time. Meghan Leahy writes, "Parental over-involvement in homework handicaps children." The parents' attitude should always be, "You can do it! Don't give up!"[4]

Another reason not to do any homework for your kid is that you may not be competent to help. The reality is that your math, writing, and grammar skills may be weak or outdated. The way the subjects are taught today may differ markedly from how you were taught when you were in school.

6. NEVER CRITICIZE A CHILD WHEN HE IS STRUGGLING

When your child is struggling, it is vital to tell him that you are proud of him for trying hard, for struggling tenaciously, and for not giving up. Criticizing him when he is struggling will achieve nothing except resentment, a dislike of learning, and parent/child conflict. Keep a positive, cheerful, upbeat attitude.

7. TELL THE TEACHER IF HOMEWORK PROBLEMS PERSIST

If your child seems to be getting overwhelmed with homework, then it is time to talk with the teacher to make him aware that there's a problem. Your child may have a learning disability or simply be missing key knowledge from an earlier grade. The latter can be addressed through extra tutoring.

Or perhaps the assignments really are too difficult. Check with other parents to see how their kids are doing. If many of the kids are feeling overwhelmed, then talk with the teacher to get his advice and guidance.

8. HELP YOUR CHILD TO BE A LEARNER RATHER THAN A GRADE GRUBBER

If you can help your child to view homework as a joyful, fun, and satisfying experience, rather than a grim, painful chore, you will have achieved something uncommon and special. Ideally your child will want to do homework for the enjoyment of learning. Obtaining a good grade will be the icing on the cake.

This is not easy to accomplish, especially at the high school level, where the workload is intense, and students are exhausted and stressed. It is tempting for your child to become a grade grubber—a student who is focused not on learning but solely on grades.

A grade grubber wants to know why she didn't get an A on an exam. With relentless vehemence, she will argue with the teacher about it, or—even worse—get her parent to do so. In contrast, a top student will ask what she can do to improve her work to become an A student, and then do it.

9. ENSURE THAT YOUR CHILD HAS TIME TO PLAY AND RELAX

As a parent, you need to ensure that your child has a balanced life, one that is not dominated by hours of homework at the exclusion of other things. Children need downtime to be creative, to exercise, to stretch, to see friends, to get outside, to connect with nature, and simply to relax.

* * *

It will always be tempting for children to avoid doing homework and instead check their Facebook page, watch TV, or distract themselves in some other way.

TAM SACKMAN

I grew up in an unusual household, because my mother worked and my father was a stay-at-home dad. I think his influence made me a more confident, well-rounded person, as well as an independent thinker and doer.

When I was five, I had a placemat with all of the presidents shown on it. Every night, my dad would quiz me on who the presidents were until I accidentally had them memorized. It became a fun party trick for him to have his five-year-old name all the presidents, but for me it was the beginning of looking at learning in a way that was fun. Because I loved learning so much (something that came from both of my parents but also seemed to be innate), they never really had to worry about whether I would do my homework or perform well in school. It's not that I wanted to impress them. I wanted to feel accomplished for myself and I did so by getting good grades.

More than in the classroom though, my father allowed me to explore any possible interest in a way that was really constructive. I once mentioned that I wanted to try archery. The next day there was a bale of hay in my backyard and a bow and arrow. I wanted a pet? He built a guinea pig hutch in our backyard. Guitar? He signed me up for lessons with the best guitar player in town. Baseball (*not* softball)? He fought the rules so that I could be the only girl on the boys' baseball team. Even when I decided that some of these pursuits were not for me, he encouraged me to follow through with them.

Your job as a parent is to do everything you can to ensure homework has a high priority in the family and gets done. With encouragement and patience, and with you modeling good work habits of your own, your kids will grow into doing homework responsibly.

* * *

JENNY PALMER

My dad definitely set high expectations, and was always happy when I did well. If I didn't have straight As, he would ask me what happened. But as long as I worked hard and tried my best, he would tell me that a B (or C!) didn't matter at all. And no matter the grade, he would still praise me for working hard and trying my best. This continued all the way through law school!

Attaching a high priority to homework means that, when it comes to tests and exams, your child will be more likely to succeed and get acceptable grades. The next chapter looks more broadly at how to help children prepare for tests and exams.

Chapter 15

Help Prepare Your Child for Tests

As a parent, you play a significant role in supporting your child when he takes tests. Even more important, you can support the daily practices that will help him know how to prepare for tests.

Encourage your child to spend time studying, and teach him good study skills. One key skill, for example, is to study every day as a test approaches rather than frantically cramming the night before.

Planning ahead and being organized are teachable skills. Disorganization can cause poor test results. Without parental encouragement, kids often struggle to be organized, and to stay motivated to be organized.

SARA PEREIRA DA SILVA

In my teens, I attended a vocational dance school, where I had both academic and artistic training. A considerable number of students suffered from some type of eating disorder, such as bulimia and anorexia. The course load was intense and I would get home around nine or ten in the evening. My father would always wait for me to have dinner so he could control what I ate. He would also make sure there was always lettuce salad for me.

On the days of my ballet public exams, my father would get more nervous than I. Sitting in the audience, he would be sweating and making faces to remind me to breathe. The trust he had in me helped me to grow up very confident about myself.

Parenting expert Amy Morin says that children usually strive to live up to their parents' expectations. She writes, "Positive expectations are contagious. If you expect your child to do well academically, he's likely to establish high expectations of himself. When children have higher expectations about their grades and academic success, they're more likely to put in the time and effort necessary to do well."[1]

Your child is likely to feel confident about taking tests if you have done everything possible throughout the school year to maximize his learning. This includes:

1. Helping him follow directions carefully

2. Encouraging him to read and to constantly enrich his vocabulary

3. Creating an atmosphere in the house where studying and doing homework are encouraged

4. Encouraging good study habits and an enthusiastic attitude about learning

5. Communicating high expectations about his work and study habits

6. Assisting with homework without actually doing it for her

7. Ensuring she gets all her homework assignments done

8. Communicating regularly with her teachers

9. Ensuring that she attends school every day

10. Helping her to be highly selective about what to watch on TV

11. Preventing her brain from being hijacked by screens

If your child finds taking tests to be particularly challenging, ask the teacher or librarian for sample tests she can use to practice answering test questions. An added benefit of studying for tests at home and taking sample tests is that it provides an opportunity for your child to repeat information taught in school, thus supporting mastery of the material.

Amy Morin encourages parents to point out to their kids that increased effort increases the likelihood of success. She writes, "Help your child recognize how more time spent studying increases the chances of doing well on a test. When kids recognize the control they have over their academic success, it motivates them to try hard."[2]

RICK STACK

Among my mother's special gifts was her boundless energy/enthusiasm/encouragement, a Jewish joie de vivre. Her *ruach* (Hebrew for spirit) instilled in me the confidence to conquer challenges. A lesson I've learned through the years is that confidence can be the secret sauce that ensures success. It is the essential ingredient I bake into my parenting, teaching, coaching, and advising.

I was lucky enough to grow up in a home that embraced my grandmother, my mother's mother, as well. She was the most positive person in my life. I'll share a couple of her witticisms:

"Look for the best in others and that's what they'll see in you." She knew it was far too easy to find fault in people. This could lead to being mired in their misery. Dig deeper, she'd insist, until you can bring out what makes the other shine.

"Might as well be happy. It costs the same." This was my grandmother's take on free will.

Test results can be heavily shaped by your child's behavior in class, and particularly by her degree of participation. The following participatory behaviors are highly desirable in class. You can talk about them with your child and underscore their importance:

- Seeking help
- Asking questions
- Paying attention
- Listening
- Following directions
- Focusing on a single task for an extended period
- Responding to questions from the teacher
- Making productive use of class time
- Participating in group discussions

- Interacting calmly with other students during class discussions
- Coping with disappointments, but still persevering.

Participating in class provides kids with an important opportunity for learning new skills. If your child comes home with low test scores, ask the teacher if he is participating in class at an acceptable level.

The night before a test, make sure your child gets a good night's sleep. On the morning of the test, assure that she eats a nutritious breakfast. This will help her perform at her best. It is hard to excel if you are tired or hungry.

Also make sure your child has all the tools he needs for the test, such as paper, pencils, and a calculator. Some schools supply them, while others may require that students bring those items themselves.

On the day of the test, be a good role model for your child. Stay calm and relaxed and exude an enthusiastic, positive mood. If you are nervous, anxious, and apprehensive, your child is likely to feel the same way. If your child is feeling anxious, help her practice relaxation techniques such as deep breathing, meditation, and stretching.

Sleep and stress are such important factors in test-taking that they deserve more discussion.

GETTING ENOUGH SLEEP

Lack of sleep can contribute to lack of attention and concentration in class, and thus to poor test results. Here are some suggestions for helping your child get more sleep.

First, model healthy sleep habits. Practice what you preach because kids will do as you do, not as you say. Parents who make sleep a priority for themselves show their children that getting enough sleep is as important as eating healthily and exercising regularly.

Second, don't allow your kids, especially young ones, to be exposed to violent media (movies, videos, TV shows, video games, online content, etc.). These can lead to anxiety and nightmares.

Third, don't allow television in the child's bedroom because watching TV will stop him from sleeping well. Also discourage screen time right before bed. The hour before bed should be for winding down, and be screen-free if possible. Unplugging before bed helps kids disconnect from the crises, anxieties, thrills, and commotion of their online lives.

Fourth, confine online activity to common areas, such as the living room. Have kids charge their phones in the common areas as well. The bedroom should be a no-connection area. Phones should be left in the living room or kitchen for the night.

Fifth, encourage physical activity after school because it helps kids sleep better. Don't let them immediately veg out in front of a screen as soon as they get home.

Sixth, discourage your child from eating close to bedtime, especially sugary treats and snacks.

And finally, encourage your child to go to bed at the same time each night, including weekends, if possible. If a child's sleep schedule changes radically at the weekend (e.g., sleeping into the afternoon), it will be very challenging for him to get back to a healthy sleep pattern starting on Sunday night.

One major reason kids don't sleep well is the pressure they feel to stay connected to their social media accounts. If your child has a heavy emotional investment in her online identities on Facebook, and so on, she will be highly tempted to stay up extremely late—perhaps half the night—logging many hours on screen. The result is severe sleep deprivation. Many studies have shown that heavy social media use by kids leads not only to poor sleep but also to lower self-esteem and higher levels of anxiety and depression.

SCOTT TALAN

My mother relocated our family to be near Acalanes High School, as my brother Steve and I were slow movers in the morning. She wanted us to be able to walk to school in less than five minutes so that the odds were better that we'd make it by first bell. She would make eggs and bacon for breakfast if time permitted. If not, cereal is what we got. If time was really tight, then we got no food at all! That was OK, as the primary goal was getting us to school on time. This focus and her flexibility made an impact on me then and still does today.

DEALING WITH DAMAGING STRESS

Your child should not avoid all stress. Stress arising from challenging situations that he can successfully handle is perfectly acceptable and healthy.

Stress prompts the body to produce adrenaline and the stress hormone cortisol. In short bursts, these hormones raise our performance and increase our capabilities, which is good. But over the long term, prolonged and excessive stress can be damaging.

Unfortunately, school leads many children to experience damaging stress. Vicki Abeles, author of *Beyond Measure: Rescuing an Overscheduled, Overtested, Underestimated Generation*, writes that there is a "nationwide epidemic of school-related stress." She says that "expectations surrounding education have spun out of control," with excessive loads of activities, homework, music, and sports. This is making children sick with stress.[3]

In place of the race for credentials, Abeles argues that parents and teachers need to "cultivate deep learning, integrity, purpose, and personal connection."[4] The goal should be learning, creativity, and curiosity rather than academic achievements, as reflected in the Harvard-or-bust mentality. Doing well in tests is important, but not at the expense of your child's health.

When talking with your child about tests, underscore that the test result is less important than the learning that happens as a result of studying for the test.

Also underscore that you love your child no matter what test scores she gets, and that you admire and respect her for the effort she is making and the grit she is showing to tackle her academic challenges.

* * *

Harmful stress from excessive homework, tests, and extracurricular activities is challenging enough to deal with. A lot of kids also have to deal with bullying, cyberbullying, intimidation, and sexual harassment. That is the focus of the next chapter.

Chapter 16

Help Kids Resist Bullying

You and your child's teachers have a major role to play in preventing bullying. Every year, millions of children are victimized by bullies at school. According to the U.S. Department of Health and Human Services, up to one in five kids is bullied and about the same number admit to bullying.[1] Sadly, bullying is common in school from kindergarten to twelfth grade.

Some studies show that one in three teenagers has been a victim of cyberbullying, which is bullying that uses electronic media to send intimidating, harassing, or threatening messages, often anonymously.

Bullying can be highly damaging to your child. It can negatively affect her ability to succeed in school. What's more, a 2016 study in the *Journal of the American Medical Association* revealed that the effects of being bullied by peers as a child or adolescent are direct, toxic, and enduring. When they reach adulthood, victims were more likely to suffer from anxiety, depression, and feeling unsafe in public places (agoraphobia).[2]

Let's look at bullying first, and then examine its nasty technical cousin, cyberbullying.

WHAT PARENTS CAN DO ABOUT BULLYING

Bullying can be physical (e.g., hitting, punching, and shoving); emotional (e.g., stalking, harassing, and shunning); or verbal (e.g., name calling, hurtful teasing, spreading lies, and gossip). These three areas obviously overlap.

Children can be victimized for many reasons. They might be overly sensitive, short, loners, obese, passive, introverted, or socially awkward at making friends. Or they might have some disability, an idiosyncrasy, an unusual characteristic, a strange last name, a stammer, or even a very sweet nature. Bullies are drawn to attack people they perceive as easy targets and vulnerable in some way. They gain self-esteem by victimizing and tormenting others.

KENT WAGNER

When I was setting out for college, my folks gave me perhaps the greatest gift a parent can offer a young college bound teenager—and I'm not sure I fully recognized it at the time.

What they gave me was encouragement and the room to make mistakes.

I was pursuing music performance, a course of study with a notoriously low earning potential. They knew I was passionate about it and their support made all the difference to me. But it was not unconditional. They are practical people; I had to continue to prove to them that I was serious, and had to maintain excellent grades.

Though we had several discussions about things like "employability" and "return on investment," these were not too serious in tone. They never tried to talk me out of wanting to make a career in music. We've discussed it since, and they say that they simply wanted me to be happy—in both the short and long term.

I've been lucky. It turned out well, and I'll always be immensely grateful to my parents for their simple encouragement.

Here are some things that you can do about it.

1. Teach your child what bullying is and that intentionally aggressive behavior toward another person is wrong. Teach him the golden rule, to treat others as he would like to be treated. Explain to him the value of empathy. A kid who has empathy and emotional intelligence will be able to understand the hurt and harm that bullying can cause. That child is more likely to speak out against it rather than being a bully, a passive bystander, or a victim. Empathy is one of the key markers for success in life.

2. Model good behavior yourself. Don't gossip, mock people, be harsh to others, deliberately hurt others, encourage cliques, or try to intimidate other people.

3. Do not shield your child from difficult and challenging situations. Shielding her can make her vulnerable to bullies. If you are an anxious,

overprotective parent, your child may also learn to be anxious and fearful. Bullies quickly zero in on such kids as easy targets.

Instead, let her learn how to deal with difficult people and situations. Show you have confidence in her. Let her take risks, make mistakes, experience frustration and anger, and even get hurt. Experiencing setbacks and then overcoming them helps a child learn to be strong, resilient, and self-confident, the very attributes that repel bullies.

4. Teach your child what to do if he observes hurtful behavior in other kids. He should alert a teacher, so that the teacher can intervene, hopefully without your child looking like a tattletale.

5. Develop good communications with your child. Talk to her everyday about what is going on in school, what went well, and what went wrong. Be alert to changes in your child's behavior and level of happiness. Look for signs that she may be being bullied. Is she afraid to attend school? Is she aggressive? Does she appear anxious?

6. Teach your child what to do if he is bullied. You or your child should alert the teacher and seek the teacher's advice and guidance. Teach your child that he is not powerless. He has control over how he reacts and responds to the bully. Teach him (perhaps with the help of role-playing) to take a stand against the bully and to be forcefully assertive. Acknowledge and validate the roiling anger and frustration inside him. He needs to hear you (and his teacher) say, "Bullying is wrong and must be stopped. There is nothing wrong with you. The person with the problem is the bully. We are with you. You are not alone. Things are not hopeless."

7. Share stories from others (e.g., friends, siblings, and neighbors) about how they dealt with the stress and trauma of bullying and what worked effectively for them. One tactic that sometimes helps is for the victim to be brave, put on a courageous face, and not look intimidated, even though he feels afraid. In a loud, firm voice, tell the bully to stop. For example, "Don't do that. I don't like it. I'll report it if you keep doing it." Then walk away and ignore the bully. While self-defense is good (including learning how to block a punch and use your voice in powerful ways), hitting back is not a good idea because the authorities might not realize your child's actions were purely defensive.

8. Encourage your school to implement school-wide programs to discourage bullying. Write to the school principal and counselor about your concerns and about your desire for a strong anti-bullying school policy and curriculum. Schools have an ethical, often legal, responsibility to keep children safe when in their care. More broadly, a student graduating from high

school should not be considered well educated unless she has developed a strong sense of responsibility for the health and welfare of other people. Kindness, respect, and cooperation should be considered as important as reading, writing, and math. The school curriculum should include teaching kids how to behave with consideration toward others, how to collaborate and get along, how to intervene on behalf of someone getting bullied, and how to stand up for what is decent and honorable. Awareness of bullying should be as much as a part of the school culture as football and baseball.

PHIL WARBURG

Nana, my grandmother, was no intellectual paragon. Abridged books published by *Reader's Digest* were stacked by her favorite upholstered chair in my family's study, alongside her ever-present knitting. I don't recall her ever reading or commenting on the *New York Times*, which always had an honored place at our breakfast table. (Yes, many people in the 1960s actually read printed newspapers!)

But she was my steadfast tutor throughout elementary and middle school, rehearsing me tirelessly on Latin conjugations, French *dictées*, English grammar, public speaking, and spelling. When I came home from school, she was the first to ask how I did on my quizzes and tests. She was always there, showing pride in my successes and lending support and encouragement when I needed to dig deeper into subjects that I had stumbled on.

Nana often complained about the darning of socks, or the fixing of zippers on our winter coats. "That's the darnedest job I've ever done!" was her earnest refrain, no pun intended or perceived. But I never, ever heard her grumble about helping my brother, two sisters, or me with our homework. It was part of the day's cadence, and it was a beautiful time spent with each of us. She made learning a collaborative effort, a family moment, fun, as well as a challenge.

WHAT PARENTS CAN DO ABOUT CYBERBULLYING

The Internet has worsened bullying and created a new, ugly, and pitiless phenomenon called cyberbullying. Cyberbullying is harder to deal with than traditional bullying because:

- Victims often have no idea who their tormentors are; it is hard to determine who is doing the bullying;

- Cyberbullies often feel anonymous and therefore unrestrained and free to be bilious and hurtful;

- Victims can never get away from the hateful and cruel messages, even after they get home from school;

- The inability to escape from cyberbullies means that the damage and stress felt by victims can be more severe;

- The usually large number of people who know about the attacks and humiliation can lead to profound feelings of embarrassment and hopelessness.

Cyberbullying expert Sherri Gordon writes that the "consequences of bullying and shaming are often unseen online. For this reason, people fail to see that they are doing anything wrong online when they hurt other people."[3]
Here are some things that you can do.

1. Be alert to potential warning signs (e.g., lower grades or avoiding school activities) that might indicate your child is being cyberbullied. It is often highly embarrassing, so victims often will try to hide their suffering and not tell anyone.

2. Talk to your child about what is happening, what might have caused the attack, and who might be behind it. Let your child know it is not her fault and that you will support and help her. Brainstorm constructive actions that you and your child can take.

3. Document the attack. Print out or take a screenshot of all the cruel messages on social media or whatever their delivery mechanism, so you and your child can show them to the school principal and counselor. This will also be useful if legal action of some kind becomes necessary.

4. Assist your child in blocking the cyberbully in whatever ways you can on your child's phone, email, and social media pages. Ask your child to change all his passwords and keep them confidential.

5. Talk to your family cell phone provider to find out if it has any tools that parents can use to help in this kind of fraught situation (e.g., blocking messages from specific senders).

* * *

If you are a parent of a girl, you have a special responsibility to help her deal with bullying and cyberbullying in the form of sexism and sexual harassment.

It's a generalization, but girls are often socialized to be nice, polite, helpful, and accommodating. Under the wrong circumstances, this can be dangerous. When a girl is harassed, bullied, or objectified in any way, she needs to fight that socialization and say, "No."

Having the capability and confidence to say "No" in certain situations is a vital skill for girls to have. You (and schools, too) should provide coaching to your daughter on how to say "No" without feeling awkward, embarrassed, or self-conscious. Sexual harassment has nothing to do with romance and everything to do with bullying and oppression. Being able to speak effectively and powerfully to stop any situation before it gets out of control is important.

Self-defense classes can be extremely helpful. Sociologist Jocelyn Hollander found that a much lower percentage of the women (all college students) who took a ten-week self-defense training class reported incidents of unwanted sexual contact compared with the women who did not take the class.[4]

Hollander found that more important than the physical defense is that most effective self-defense classes for women and girls also teach students how to set boundaries. When dealing with obnoxious or harassing behavior, setting boundaries is important, and saying "No" is a key tool.

ALEXANDRIA WARD

The most exciting part of the day was when my dad came home from work.

As soon as I heard the garage door opening I would tear through the house and eagerly stash myself in some hiding place. Most often I would hide behind the door of the garage, the door my dad had to come through when he entered the house. When the door opened it would create a triangular space in the corner of the laundry room, the perfect hiding spot. I hid, of course, so that my dad would find me, and it was ridiculously exciting to hide and hear him looking for me.

All my life my dad worked long hours. First, he was a manager at McDonald's, then he was a real estate agent. When I was about seven, he bought an old newspaper printing shop in central Houston and opened a plumbing supply store there. Opening your own business is no easy feat. My father worked innumerable hours at the store, seven days a week, for years. Needless to say I did not get to spend a lot of time with him growing up.

But just because you do not see something does not mean that it is not influencing the life around you. Gravity holds things down on earth. The crew supports the cast in a play or a film. My dad enabled me to achieve the success I have had so far. I am a first-generation college student, and I have had such a wonderful life. My mother built and maintained the home and my father provided the ability for her to do that. Going to college, going to graduate school, studying abroad in France, all would have been incredibly difficult and far more stressful without the support of my father.

On occasion my dad tells me that he is proud of me. He is not a particularly affectionate or emotionally expressive man, and when he lets me know that I've done something to make him proud, it warms my heart in a way nothing else can. It gives me strength to know that whatever I am doing, wherever I am, my father is supporting me. Thinking about the way he worked so hard to build his business and provide for his family is inspiring. It makes me want to work harder, to show my dad that I value hard work, and I value my dad.

* * *

Bullying in its various poisonous incarnations can be a major challenge to you in your mission to help your child do well in school. But it is really part of a much bigger problem. Children today are being brought up in a toxic, sexualized, and violent culture that is inimical to most values espoused by parents, teachers, and schools. How to deal with this problem is the topic of the next chapter.

Chapter 17

Counter a Toxic, Sexualized, and Violent Culture

In 1987, Tipper Gore wrote *Raising PG Kids in an X-Rated Society*, a book about how explicit sex and graphic violence was being fed to children by an immoral entertainment media industry eager to make money at the expense of vulnerable children.[1]

Gore was particularly incensed about how the industry, showing no self-restraint, was glamorizing explicit images of sex and violence to younger and younger kids. She argued persuasively that children deserve "vigilant protection from the excesses of adult society."[2]

Unfortunately, the excesses have gotten far worse since Tipper Gore's book was published. That's because of the relentless invasion of screens permeating every aspect of our lives, and because films and other media themselves have become more graphic. A 2013 report from the American Academy of Pediatrics (AAP) found that violence in films has more than doubled since 1950, and gun violence in PG-13 films has more than tripled since Gore's book was published.[3] It has also become scarily realistic.

SAM WHITCRAFT

Throughout my career, a skill that has served me well is my comfort with public speaking. As a conservation biologist, advocate, and educator, being able to speak to a class or conference about a subject in a way that is engaging and meaningful has made all the difference. I have presented to eager students and angry fishermen alike, and have always found a way to be persuasive.

I can attest to the fact that this all started with my mom coaching me every night for two weeks for a middle school speech contest. First she helped by guiding me to pick an appropriate quotation to build my speech around. She knew my love of Shakespeare, and together we chose,

"This above all: to thine own self be true, And it must follow, as the night the day, Thou canst not then be false to any man."—*Hamlet*

Finding that theme inspired me to try to write and give a speech worthy of the quotation. I'm sure she knew that.

I wrote a first draft that was very rough. My mom made suggestions that helped me as I rewrote it several times. This was when I learned that good writing is in the third or fourth draft—another valuable lesson. She suggested that I think of examples the audience, the students at my school, could relate to. In response to that suggestion, I incorporated mentions of the struggles and success of the cast of the school play, and our pride in our underdog but undefeated football team.

She helped me figure out the pacing and storytelling. But, most important, she had me practice the speech several times every night. It was frustrating as she constantly reminded me to slow down, to speak clearly and deliberately. I learned to pause between key ideas, and tell a compelling story.

When it came time to give my speech in front of the whole school, I was nervous but felt prepared. I had practiced with my mom so many times, I almost didn't need the note cards we had so meticulously compiled together. I gave the speech, and when it ended I was rewarded with a resounding applause. I won the speech contest, which at our school was a high honor.

I also used the written speech as part of my application to a very competitive boarding school, and was accepted.

My mother's patient, persistent guidance and coaching truly helped me thrive in school and beyond.

Media violence and graphic sex affect kids in every aspect of their lives, including in the classroom. They distract kids when in school, causing fear and anxiety that hinder children's ability to focus and learn, and to grow into confident, grounded, and caring members of society.

As a parent, you are faced with the daunting task of protecting your child from terrifying, sordid, creepy material while he is flooded with a tidal wave of alluring television programs, movies, video games, videos, and social media sites, much of which contain such material. Author Stephen R. Covey once wrote, "In many ways, television is like an open sewer pipe right into a family, just pouring out unwanted images and feelings."[4] And he wrote that in 1997—a more innocent time. Porn-level sex in mainstream TV is now common.

Many studies show that kids who watch media violence are prone to reduced empathy, increased aggression, and other disruptive behaviors that can fetter their success in school, to say nothing of giving them nightmares, anxieties, and terrifying thoughts. Seemingly small experiences can have a severe and enduring impact. For example, imagine the trauma to a ten-year-old kid when shown a trailer (perhaps by an unthinking or trouble-making older friend or sibling) for a horror movie depicting graphic, sexual violence and gratuitous, sadistic torture.

It is virtually impossible to prevent children from being exposed to content that will traumatize them, especially if they visit a friend's house where the parents have permissive standards. The content that some parents will allow even young children to see is astonishing. Kids should not be deprived of their childhood in that way.

Here are some steps that you can take to protect your child from inappropriate, scary, and graphic material and to limit her exposure to mature content.

1. Watch out for misleading ratings, also known as "ratings creep." What once might have received an R rating might now get a PG-13 or even a PG rating. Just because a movie has a PG rating doesn't mean it is going to be suitable for your child to see. Check out Common Sense Media's age ratings, as well as its detailed information on the type and quantity of violence and explicit sexual content in a movie or television show.[5]

   If you're not sure, screen the movie or TV show before letting your child watch it, or watch it with him and talk about it, looking for teachable moments. The same goes for websites and video games. Check them out yourself before allowing your child to experience them.

   Other parents can also be useful sources of guidance if they share your standards regarding what is healthy and unhealthy for kids to watch.

2. If your child seems troubled about something, it may be that a friend has shared scary videos, movies, or video games with him. The friend may have parents who are too preoccupied with other concerns to even know how much graphic violence and explicit sex their child sees. You may need to talk to those parents, or find ways to help your child find new, less harmful friends.

3. Cut back on screen time. Many studies have shown that reduced screen time leads to kids being less anxious, doing better in school, sleeping

better, and being healthier. This is especially true if they replace screen time with getting outside, spending time in nature, and interacting face-to-face with their families.

The key is for you to be strong and refuse to give in to temper tantrums and threats from a child who wants to watch something inappropriate. When you know that she will be deeply upset, distressed, and disturbed by whatever it is she wants to see, then you must be firm.

This is a good opportunity to teach your child about the importance of resisting peer pressure. The craving to see an inappropriate program or play a violent video game is likely to be because friends are doing so. Don't succumb to pressure. Set an example of strength and grit.

Explain that violence and other inappropriate, grown-up content is harmful for children and that a parent's responsibility is to protect his child from content that will hurt and traumatize her. Dr. Leonard Sax writes in *The Collapse of Parenting*, "It's tough to be a parent in a culture that constantly undermines parental authority," but good parents are resolute and authoritative.[6] That is their job.

4. Look for movies and other media that have positive messages and that can build your child's characters, life skills, and such positive values as bravery, gratitude, honesty, empathy, diligence, and persistence. Again, Common Sense Media and similar sites can help you identify such films, websites, and video games.[7] Much of what is popular on TV encourages meanness, aggression, coarseness, self-absorption, immediate gratification, indolence, disrespect, vulgarity, and raunchiness. But you can find good material out there if you look for it. Teach kids to be media savvy.

5. Compliment your children (and this applies especially to girls) on their academic performance, generosity, diligence, conscientiousness, and compassion, not only on their looks. It's nice for a daughter to know that her mom and dad think she is beautiful, but you need to go out of your way to put a lot more emphasis on her mind, character, values, and behavior. The same goes for boys, of course.

Digital technology sends many harmful and toxic messages to kids about their appearance, giving it far too much emphasis, and neglecting to stress the importance of people's talents, capabilities, character, leadership abilities, and what they can accomplish. Girls especially are under attack, but both boys and girls should focus on being strong, fit and healthy, not on what they look like. An unhealthy preoccupation with physical appearance is harmful.

CARLTON JOHN WILLEY

My parents created an environment in which I had every opportunity and motivation to thrive. Most essential is the fact that they provided a loving and stable home, free from concerns about survival, safety, adequate food, and shelter. Because these essential needs were consistently met, I was able to direct my efforts toward achieving in both academic and extracurricular areas.

My parents read to me on a daily basis when I was young. Conversation was also a skill that I developed in early life. My mother was a stay-at-home until I was five years old. She would talk to me whenever we were together, asking questions about what I was doing, thinking, or feeling. I rarely had a babysitter and I rarely watched television. I went with mom to do the shopping and carpooling for my four siblings, which provided lots of time to talk. As a family, almost every weekend we would have an outing that was both fun and educational.

From my father I learned that, when mechanical things break, it is fun to take them apart, figure out what was wrong, and try to fix them. If something broke at our house, we didn't wait for someone to come fix it; we did it ourselves.

My parents were active in the PTA and never missed a "Meet the Teacher Night" or parent/teacher conference. As the youngest of five children, I was constantly aware that our family put a high value on education, and had high expectations. The halo effect of having all of my siblings in the gifted program was very real to me. The teachers that had my older siblings expected excellence from me, much more than from my average classmates, and I didn't want to let them down. We were profusely praised by our parents for our accomplishments, complete with ice cream outings for the entire family to celebrate the latest award or recognition.

In summary, I believe my successes stem from developing in a loving, nurturing, healthy, competitive, stable environment in which education was revered and high achievement was expected.

* * *

Porn deserves special mention because kids are getting exposed to it at shockingly young ages. It can disrupt and obstruct children's desire to do well in school. In her book *American Girls: Social Media and the Secret Lives of Teenagers*, Nancy Jo Sales reveals that children are being exposed increasingly to pornography online. What is even more alarming to her is that much of the sexual content they see contains violence against women, violence "in which men dominate and control women, insult them, and sometimes hurt them physically."[8]

Sociologist Gail Dines reports that a 2010 meta-analysis of several studies found "an overall significant positive association between pornography use and attitudes supporting violence against women."[9] Online porn is also giving children some very disturbing ideas about how they are supposed to behave and appear.

Another area deserving special mention is the sexualization of girls at increasingly young ages. Sexualization and sexuality are distinct. As Dr. Leonard Sax explains in *Girls on the Edge*, "Sexuality is good, but *sexualization* is bad. Sexuality is about your identity as a woman or as a man, about feeling sexual. That's a healthy part of being human. . . . But *sexualization* is about being an object for the pleasure of others, about being on display for others. Sexuality is about who you are. Sexualization is about how you look."[10]

In *American Girls* Nancy Jo Sales depicts the highly sexualized environment in which children are mired today on the screens and digital platforms that absorb their attention. She stresses that younger and younger kids are being exposed to overtly sexual content on the web, including sexually exploitative material.[11] Popular culture focuses attention on the kids who dress in hyper-sexualized ways.

Sexualization is an impediment to kids succeeding in school. When kids who are heavy consumers of popular culture are in school, they are likely to be thinking about sexually exploitative images instead of science or history or French. Girls especially are being encouraged by popular culture to present themselves as sex objects in order to please boys, when they should be focused on their studies and on learning.

MACKENZIE YARYURA

When I think about the ways in which my parents helped me thrive in school, the word that comes to mind is *presence*. From listening to how my day went when I came home from school, to going to "Back to School Night," to attending every academic competition, my parents made a point to schedule around school.

My first memory of this is from when I was in fourth grade. I loved math; the concept of simplification, discovering an unknown "x," and having one right answer was very stimulating. However, math is not a subject that comes easily to all elementary students, and the teachers did not have the bandwidth to challenge those of us who were really excited about the subject. Instead of just giving me extra problems at home, my mom made an effort to come to the school every Friday to teach advanced mathematical problem solving to a group of kids. It was important for me to see my mom at my school, supporting the teachers and creating opportunities for my classmates and me to be challenged. If my mom thought it was worth the time to be in my elementary school, then it must be a pretty special place.

Although my dad was at work most days, he would always ask questions about what I learned, and what I still didn't know. When it came time to perform, such as in the county-wide elementary school math competition, both of my parents were there to support me. Throughout middle and high school, my mom was always finding ways to create additional opportunity for me within the school system. My dad was always reminding me of how much I knew, and pushing me to think about how much I had yet to learn. It was clear that succeeding in school was a family priority, and that they were willing to invest their own time and energy to support me in my academic endeavors.

Dr. Leonard Sax writes in *Girls on the Edge*, "If your daughter can develop a sense of self that is deeply rooted, then she will grow up to be a resilient and self-confident woman. . . . A sense of self is about who you *are*, not about how you look."[12] Who you are is far more important than what you look like.

The entertainment industry, as Tipper Gore pointed out years ago, should create a media environment and digital content where kids see healthy media images of themselves and positive role models to which they can aspire. Today's kids are exposed to massive amounts of sexualized content through advertisements, reality television, PG-13 and R-rated movies, music videos, the Internet, social media, and video games. Sexually suggestive material encourages sexualized talk and behavior, none of which helps kids to succeed in school.

Don't let your child watch programs with disturbing violence or inappropriate sexuality. Don't let him watch shows that glamorize alcohol and drugs or that have too many commercials (which stimulate greed and acquisitiveness). Beware, too, of music videos because of the raunchy lyrics and inappropriate sexuality.

When your child reaches the age of about ten, you need to move from a posture of banning material to explaining why it is harmful. You can't protect your child forever. Teaching must eventually replace censorship as your child grows up. Talk with your teenager about the media he wants to consume. Eventually the education and judgment you instill in him must take over.

In 1994, Dr. Mary Pipher wrote in *Reviving Ophelia*, "The way the media have dehumanized sex and fostered violence should be a topic of a national debate."[13] The need for such a debate has become blisteringly obvious today, when popular culture, exacerbated by an explosion of screens, has worsened and become intensely toxic.

It is not good enough for you to take a laissez-faire attitude toward media. Children today routinely access online adult material, attend adult concerts, and watch adult TV programs that glamorize casual sex, violence, drug use, consumerism, depravity, and promiscuity. You are facing the tough and vexing challenge of how to protect your child from this material and the harm it can cause.

* * *

The next and final chapter focuses on the bigger picture. Why is the content of this book important? Is it because doing well in school will get you into a good college, followed by a well-paying job and a successful career? The short answer, as you will see, is no.

Chapter 18

See the Bigger Picture

This book focuses on effective parenting and on how you can help your child succeed. Why is that important? The answer might seem obvious. You want him to work hard and get high grades in school, so he can get into a good college, and then get a decent job and have a comfortable life. Many parents assume high grades show that their kids are succeeding in school.

But you also want your child to live a fulfilling, responsible, and meaningful life helping others and contributing to society, perhaps even advancing a great cause.

How can you help her focus on deep learning, personal development, building relationships, and acquiring integrity, purpose, courage, creativity, and curiosity, instead of just getting good grades and high test scores?

Getting top grades and test scores isn't necessarily going to help your child lead a fulfilling and happy life. As Dr. Leonard Sax points out in *The Collapse of Parenting*, "Many of the skills needed to succeed in life are different from the skills needed for admission to a top college."[1] And professor Carol Dweck from Stanford says, "We're training kids to get As, to get the next high test score, to get into the next school, but we're not training them to be dreamers, to have some goal for their lives that will make them feel fulfilled."[2]

One of the problems with schools is that kids acquire the incentive to be cautious about their education. They are tempted not to take classes in which they might learn exciting and challenging new material, if that means taking the risk of getting a grade lower than A. "The values inculcated at most schools today . . . reinforce a reluctance to take risks, a reluctance to fail," writes Leonard Sax.[3]

But that is not good training for real life. In the wider world, you can't always play it safe. Often boldness and audacity are needed, especially in an environment where people regularly change jobs and even careers. In real life, organizations go bankrupt, people get fired and contracts fall through. If your child goes through school without experiencing setbacks and failures, then real life can be disconcerting and highly stressful for him.

Katty Kay, lead anchor of "BBC World News America" and coauthor of *The Confidence Code*, writes, "Researchers have found that it's the very process of taking risks and messing up that builds confidence. . . . We tend to make our kids' lives easy by doing things for them because we are so desperate for them to succeed. But then when you tell a child she can do 'anything,' she has no evidence to support that because she hasn't had to work hard at anything."[4]

Your child must realize that failing does not mean he is a failure. Mistakes are a normal part of life. One of the most important skills your child should have is the ability to take risks in a scary world and not fear failing. Failure is an unpleasant, but essential, part of striving and learning. To fail can mean that you are trying hard, taking risks, and getting out of your comfort zone— all necessary precursors to success. Schools are neglecting to teach real-world lessons like these. As a parent, you must step in and help by *commending* your child when he takes risks and fails.

In her book *The Gift of Failure: How the Best Parents Learn to Let Go So Their Children Can Succeed*, Jessica Lahey describes the chance for kids to experience failure as "the opportunity to solve their own problems."[5] She encourages parents to embrace their children's setbacks along with their successes.

Your child needs to experience disappointments, setbacks, and failures in order to prepare her to be resilient in the real world. Leonard Sax writes, "The humility born of failure can build growth and wisdom and an openness to new things in a way that success almost never does."[6] Encourage your child to be bold, try new things, take on challenges, and be a persevering risk taker.

For example, recommend that your child challenges authority when appropriate, rather than being obedient, docile, and doing everything needed to get an A grade. It's good to respectfully debate and disagree. Docility and "being nice" will get you high grades, but won't get you very far in life. There's a fine line between being well behaved and being meek. No one wants to hire the latter.

If your child does take risks academically, his grades might decline, but he will be better prepared to find success in life. You have a more profound responsibility than helping him to get good grades in school. You need to teach him that *character* matters more than grades, and that the deepest meaning in life is to be found, not in high grades and a comfortable job, but in the sense of profound fulfillment gained by working on issues and projects that matter and that help others.

The key is service to others and reaching your full potential as a human being. Getting As for the sake of getting As so you can get into a good college will wear thin very quickly if it isn't supported by a deeper sense of why it all matters.

The purpose of your child's school experience should not be just to get high grades. It should be to develop her character. Kids need not only good grades, but also the emotional intelligence to behave with integrity, self-control, and self-discipline. Empathy and a sense of responsibility are most important if you want your child to find profound, long-term happiness.

ALEXANDRA (ALY) YINGST

Without a doubt, my parents are the people to whom I can attribute my success in life. The best thing that they did every day after school was simply to ask about my day. Feeling that someone had a genuine interest in the minute details of my day pushed me to try a little harder each day; that way I could come home and see how proud they were of me for learning something new in school.

Reporting back on what I learned in school was probably the best possible way to review for tests, because I had to remember what I learned and had to describe it in a way that I could understand. Even when I was in high school and started to take classes on subjects my parents didn't know much about, they would listen to what I had to say.

They also realized the importance of both schoolwork and activities. I always completed my homework, but I was never forced to forfeit my extracurricular activities for the sake of having more time for homework. In this way, I was taught at a young age how to balance my time. My parents are the reason I am the person I am today, and I feel so lucky to have been raised by such wonderful people.

About twenty years ago, Neil Postman cautioned in *The End of Education* that education was being replaced by "schooling," in which learning is pursued only for its utility. He was warning that education was in danger of simply being a means to an end—gaining employment—rather than a generative process that shapes the sort of society we want to create and live in.[7]

Leonard Sax writes in *The Collapse of Parenting*, "One of your tasks as a parent is to instill a sense of meaning, a longing for something higher and deeper. Without meaning, life comes to seem pointless and futile. . . . Once children have a sense of meaning, they can pursue achievement with confidence because they know *why* that achievement is worth pursuing."[8]

In a TED talk given in November 2015 called "How to Raise Successful Kids Without Over-Parenting," educator Julie Lythcott-Haims says, "Our kids need [parents] to be a little less obsessed with grades and scores and a whole lot more interested in childhood providing a foundation for their success built on things like love and chores."[9]

This is ultimately what you need to do: help your children do well in school and as they grow up, so that they can create a life for themselves that has purpose and meaning, and that makes the world a better place.

Notes

INTRODUCTION

1. Jennifer Senior, *All Joy and No Fun: The Paradox of Modern Parenthood* (New York: HarperCollins, 2014), page 10.

CHAPTER 1

1. Jeffrey Zaslow, "Papa, Don't Preach: Why Some Fathers Don't Relate Well to Their Daughters," *Wall Street Journal*, November 6, 2003.

2. Senior, *All Joy and No Fun*, page 253.

CHAPTER 2

1. Meghan Leahy, "Five Things That Can Make You a Better Parent Right Now," *Washington Post*, July 20, 2016.

2. Stephen R. Covey, *The 7 Habits of Highly Effective Families* (New York: Golden Books, 1997), page 76.

3. David Brooks, "The Moral Bucket List," *New York Times*, April 11, 2015.

4. Dr. Leonard Sax, *The Collapse of Parenting: How We Hurt Our Kids When We Treat Them Like Grown-Ups* (New York: Basic Books, 2015), page 262.

5. Dr. Catherine Steiner-Adair, *The Big Disconnect: Protecting Childhood and Family Relationships in the Digital Age* (New York: HarperCollins, 2013), page 221.

CHAPTER 3

1. Ron Taffel, *The Second Family: How Adolescent Power Is Changing the American Family* (New York: St. Martin's, 2001).

2. Sax, *The Collapse of Parenting*, pages 18 and 19.

3. Don Dinkmeyer and Gary D. McKay, *The Parent's Handbook* (Minnesota: American Guidance Service, 1989), page 103.

4. Meghan Leahy, "Five Things That Can Make You a Better Parent Right Now," *The Washington Post*, July 20, 2016.

5. Maureen Dowd, "Getting to Know Mother by Mail," *Washington Post*, May 8, 1983.

CHAPTER 4

1. Sax, *The Collapse of Parenting*, page 125.

2. Senior, *All Joy and No Fun*, page 261.

3. Meghan Leahy, "Five Things That Can Make You a Better Parent Right Now," *Washington Post*, July 20, 2016.

4. E. J. Dionne, Jr., "What Gratitude Requires," *Washington Post*, November 28, 2013.

5. Dr. Mary Pipher, *The Shelter of Each Other: Rebuilding Our Families* (New York: G.P. Putnam's Sons, 1996), page 15.

6. Kimberly Palmer, *Smart Mom, Rich Mom: How to Build Wealth While Raising a Family* (New York: American Management Association, 2016).

CHAPTER 5

1. Sax, *The Collapse of Parenting*, page 141.

2. Sax, *The Collapse of Parenting*, page 67.

3. Sax, *The Collapse of Parenting*, page 7.

4. Switch & Shift, "Build Morale by Catching People Doing Something Right," June 12, 2014, http://switchandshift.com/build-morale-by-catching-people-doing-something-right.

5. Dinkmeyer and McKay, *The Parent's Handbook*, page 38.

6. Amy Morin, "Did You Know Harsh Discipline Turns Kids into Good Liars?" January 7, 2015, http://motherhoodinstyle.net/2015/01/07/did-you-know-harsh-discipline-turns-kids-into-good-liars/.

7. Guidance for Effective Discipline, April 2014, http://pediatrics.aappublications.org/content/101/4/723.

8. Meghan Leahy, "Spanking Doesn't Work," *Washington Post*, November 4, 2015.

CHAPTER 6

1. Carol Dweck, *Mindset: The New Psychology of Success* (New York: Ballantine Books, 2016).

2. Salman Khan, TED talk March 2011, *Let's Use Video to Reinvent Education*, https://www.ted.com/talks/salman_khan_let_s_use_video_to_reinvent_education

3. Angela Duckworth, *Grit: The Power of Passion and Perseverance* (New York: Scribner, 2016).

CHAPTER 7

1. Deborah Fox and Nadine Epstein, "Use 'Listening Time' to Maintain Emotional Connections," *Washington Post*, May 24, 1999.

2. Joe Kelly, *Dads and Daughters: How to Inspire, Understand, and Support Your Daughter When She's Growing Up So Fast* (New York: Broadway Books, 2002), page 22.

3. Mary Pipher, *Reviving Ophelia: Saving the Selves of Adolescent Girls* (New York: Ballantine Books, 1994), page 19.

4. Pipher, *Reviving Ophelia*, page 23.

5. Nancy Gruver, *How to Say It to Girls: Communicating with Your Growing Daughter* (New York: Penguin Random House, 2004).

CHAPTER 8

1. Suzanne Nelson, "Why I Let My Children Read Books About Upsetting Things," *Washington Post*, February 25, 2016.

2. Ibid.

3. Ibid.

4. Bruce Feiler, *The Secrets of Happy Families: Improve Your Mornings, Rethink Family Dinner, Fight Smarter, Go Out and Play, and Much More* (New York: HarperCollins, 2013).

CHAPTER 9

1. H. J. Press, *Science Experiments: More Than 300 Entertaining, Educational, and Easy-to-Do Projects* (New York: Sterling Publisher, 1998).

2. Richard Louv, *Last Child in the Woods: Saving Our Children from Nature-Deficit Disorder* (New York: Workman Publishing, 2008).

3. Kim John Payne, *Simplicity Parenting: Using the Extraordinary Power of Less to Raise Calmer, Happier, and More Secure Kids* (New York: Ballantine Books, 2009), page 81.

4. Jessica Pels, "Why There Are Way Too Few Girls in Tech, and How Chelsea Clinton Wants to Change It," *Teen Vogue*, June 26, 2014.

CHAPTER 10

1. Sue Shellenbarger, "Tucking the Kids In—In the Dorm: Colleges Ward Off Overinvolved Parents," *Wall Street Journal*, July 28, 2005.

2. Marilyn vos Savant, "What to Teach Your Kids Before They Leave Home," *Parade*, March 25, 2001, pages 20–21.

CHAPTER 11

1. Benjamin Stokes, email message to author, November 19, 2016.
2. Common Sense Media, *Landmark Report: U.S. Teens Use an Average of Nine Hours of Media per Day, Tweens Use Six Hours*, November 2, 2015. https://www.commonsensemedia.org/about-us/news/press-releases/landmark-report-us-teens-use-an-average-of-nine-hours-of-media-per-day.
3. Steiner-Adair, *The Big Disconnect*, page 11.
4. Steiner-Adair, *The Big Disconnect*, page 11.
5. Steiner-Adair, *The Big Disconnect*, page 16.
6. Jane Scott, "Parenting by Siri," *New York Times*, August 10, 2014.
7. Payne, *Simplicity Parenting*, page xi.
8. Meghan Leahy, "Creating a Good Boundary," *Washington Post*, June 4, 2015.
9. Common Sense Media, *Landmark Report: U.S. Teens Use an Average of Nine Hours of Media per Day, Tweens Use Six Hours*, November 2, 2015. https://www.commonsensemedia.org/about-us/news/press-releases/landmark-report-us-teens-use-an-average-of-nine-hours-of-media-per-day.
10. American Academy of Pediatrics, "American Academy of Pediatrics Announces New Recommendations for Children's Media Use," October 21, 2016, https://www.aap.org/en-us/about-the-aap/aap-press-room/pages/american-academy-of-pediatrics-announces-new-recommendations-for-childrens-media-use.aspx.
11. https://www.commonsense.org/.
12. American Academy of Pediatrics, "American Academy of Pediatrics Announces New Recommendations for Children's Media Use," October 21, 2016, https://www.aap.org/en-us/about-the-aap/aap-press-room/pages/american-academy-of-pediatrics-announces-new-recommendations-for-childrens-media-use.aspx.
13. Benjamin Stokes, email message to author, November 21, 2016.
14. Benjamin Stokes, email message to author, November 21, 2016.
15. Payne, *Simplicity Parenting*.
16. Payne, *Simplicity Parenting*, page 8.
17. Pipher, *The Shelter of Each Other*.
18. Lindsay Grace, email message to author, November 28, 2016.

CHAPTER 12

1. Chad Hayes, "Before Fixing a Problem, Figure Out What It Is," *Washington Post*, November 3, 2015.
2. Leonard Sax, *Girls on the Edge: The Four Factors Driving the New Crisis for Girls* (New York: Basic Books, 2010), page 129.
3. Sax, *Girls on the Edge*, page 130.

CHAPTER 13

1. Myra and David Sadker, *Failing at Fairness: How Our Schools Cheat Girls* (New York: Touchstone, 1994).
2. Sax, *Girls on the Edge*, page 140.
3. Pipher, *Reviving Ophelia*.

CHAPTER 14

1. National Education Association, http://www.nea.org/tools/16938.htm.
2. National Parent Teacher Association, http://www.pta.org/programs/content.cfm?ItemNumber=1730.
3. Stephen R. Covey, *The 7 Habits of Highly Effective People: Restoring the Character Ethic* (New York: Simon and Schuster, 1989).
4. Meghan Leahy, "'Should We Let Her Fail?' Might Be the Wrong Question," *Washington Post*, January 14, 2016.

CHAPTER 15

1. Amy Morin, "How Parental Expectations Affect Children's Academic Achievement," September 8, 2014, http://amymorinlcsw.com/.
2. Ibid.
3. Vicki Abeles, *Beyond Measure: Rescuing an Overscheduled, Overtested, Underestimated Generation* (New York: Simon & Schuster, 2015).
4. Ibid.

CHAPTER 16

1. U.S. Department of Health and Human Services, https://www.nichd.nih.gov/health/topics/bullying/conditioninfo/Pages/risk.aspx.
2. *Journal of the American Medical Association*, http://jamanetwork.com/journals/jamapsychiatry/article-abstract/2472952.
3. Sherri Gordon, https://www.verywell.com/sherri-gordon-bullying-expert-460467.
4. Jocelyn Hollander, "The Importance of Self-Defense Training for Sexual Violence Prevention," April 13, 2016. http://journals.sagepub.com/doi/abs/10.1177/0959353516637393.

CHAPTER 17

1. Tipper Gore, *Raising PG Kids in an X-Rated Society* (New York: Bantam Books, 1987).

2. Gore, *Raising PG Kids in an X-Rated Society,* page 27.

3. American Academy of Pediatrics, "Gun Violence Trends in Movies," November 2013, http://pediatrics.aappublications.org/content/early/2013/11/06/peds.2013-1600.

4. Covey, *The Seven Habits of Highly Effective Families*, page 124.

5. https://www.commonsense.org/.

6. Sax, *The Collapse of Parenting*, page 23.

7. https://www.commonsense.org/.

8. Nancy Jo Sales, *American Girls: Social Media and the Secret Lives of Teenagers* (New York: Knopf, 2016).

9. Gail Dines, "Is Pornography Immoral? That Doesn't Matter: It's Now a Public Health Crisis," *Washington Post*, April 10, 2016.

10. Sax, *Girls on the Edge*, pages 12–13.

11. Sales, *American Girls*.

12. Sax, *Girls on the Edge*, pages 3–4.

13. Pipher, *Reviving Ophelia*.

CHAPTER 18

1. Sax, *The Collapse of Parenting*, page 189.

2. Carol Dweck, professor of Psychology, Stanford University, as quoted in the *New York Times* on June 23, 2016.

3. Sax, *The Collapse of Parenting*, page 191.

4. Katy Kay, quoted in essay by Kristyn Kusek Lewis entitled "The Secret to Raising a Happy, Confident Girl" in *Parents Magazine*, http://www.parents.com/parenting/better-parenting/positive/the-secret-to-raising-a-happy-confident-girl/.

5. Jessica Lahey, *The Gift of Failure: How the Best Parents Learn to Let Go So Their Children Can Succeed* (New York: HarperCollins, 2015).

6. Sax, *The Collapse of Parenting*, page 191.

7. Neil Postman, *The End of Education: Redefining the Value of School* (New York: Knopf, 1995).

8. Sax, *The Collapse of Parenting*, page 195.

9. TED talk by Julie Lythcott-Haims entitled *How to Raise Successful Kids Without Over-Parenting*, filmed in November 2015.

Index

validation, 51
values, 4, 67
victimization, 113, 115
violence, 121, 123, 128;
    pornography and, 125–26;
    visuals of, 7
virtues, 14–15

Wagner, Kent, 114
Warburg, Phil, 116
Ward, Alexandria, 118–19
Whitcraft, Sam, 121–22

Willey, Carlton John, 125
wisdom, 28, 38
workaholic, ix
worth, 6, 36
writing, 6, 21–22, 71

Yaryura, Mackenzie, 126–27
yelling, 37
Yingst, Alexandra (Aly), 131
you-messages, 52

Zaslow, Jeffrey, 6

About the Author

Chris Palmer is a professor, speaker, author, and wildlife film producer who gives speeches and workshops on a variety of topics, including how to achieve success and productivity, how to parent effectively, how to motivate and engage students, and how to make wildlife films.

He is also the proud father of three successful daughters: Kimberly, Christina, and Jennifer.

His earlier books were *Shooting in the Wild* (2010), *Confessions of a Wildlife Filmmaker* (2015), and *Now What, Grad? Your Path to Success After College* (2015).

He serves on American University's full-time faculty at the School of Communication in Washington, D.C., as Distinguished Film Producer in Residence. In addition to teaching filmmaking, he teaches a class called *Design Your Life for Success.*

Born in Hong Kong, Chris grew up in England and immigrated to the United States in 1972. He has swum with dolphins and whales, come face-to-face with sharks and Kodiak bears, camped with wolf packs, and waded hip-deep through the Everglade swamps. He founded and directs AU's Center for Environmental Filmmaking. He also serves as president of the MacGillivray Freeman Films Educational Foundation, which produces and funds IMAX films, and serves on the board of ten nonprofits.

He has spearheaded the production of more than 300 hours of original programming for prime time television and the IMAX film industry, and has worked with the likes of Robert Redford, Paul Newman, Jane Fonda, and Ted Turner. He and his colleagues have won many awards, including two Emmys and an Oscar nomination.

He spent twenty-five years working for the National Audubon Society and the National Wildlife Federation in top executive positions. For five years, he was a stand-up comedian and performed regularly in DC comedy clubs. In his twenty years before becoming a film producer, Chris was a high school boxing champion, an officer in the Royal Navy, an engineer, a business consultant, an energy analyst, an environmental activist, chief energy advisor to a senior U.S. senator, and a political appointee in the Environmental Protection Agency under President Jimmy Carter. He also jumped out of helicopters and worked on an Israeli kibbutz. Chris holds three degrees from London and Harvard.

He can be reached at palmer@american.edu and at (202) 885-3408 at American University. His website is www.ChrisPalmerOnline.com. Chris encourages you to write to him with suggestions for the next edition of this book.

All proceeds from the sale of this book will go to fund scholarships for students at the American University School of Communication.